THE ART
OF
LEGACY

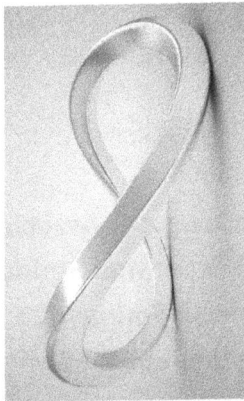

BY

DR. RUSS MOYER

Published by:

McDougal & Associates
18896 Greenwell Springs Road
Greenwell Springs, LA 70739
www.thepublishedword.com

McDougal & Associates is an organization dedicated to the spreading the Gospel of the Lord Jesus Christ to as many people as possible in the shortest time possible.

ISBN: 978-1-950398-15-7

Printed on demand in the U.S., the U.K. and Australia
For Worldwide Distribution

Presented To:

_____

By:

_____

On:

_____

Message:

_____

_____

_____

_____

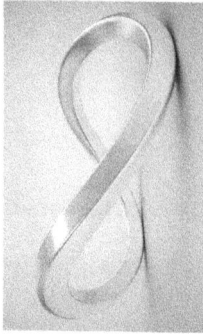

Foreword by John P. Kelly

Our Father is a generational God who wants us to pour into the lives of the next generation by preparing and equipping them to run and win their earthy race. In *The Art of Legacy*, Dr. Russ Moyer gives us a true and practical understanding of how to be good and honorable spiritual parents.

I had the honor of meeting Russ and his wife Mave in April 2004, when a group of apostolic leaders and I commissioned them both as apostolic leaders. We agreed with the call of God on their lives and His plan for them to facilitate ministry, equip the saints and add to the Kingdom of God in the Golden Horseshoe region of Ontario, Canada.

Since then, Russ and Mave have continued to be faithful to the vision of equipping and releasing, birthing and building. They have invested themselves as spiritual parents in many in the Body of Christ, those they have poured into up close and personal and many more who are ordained and credentialed in the Eagle Worldwide Network of Ministries. Countless others have been touched and blessed as the Moyers travelled and ministered prophetically and in the manifestation of the gifts of the Spirit around the world. Now, after twenty faithful and fruitful years, they are modelling passing the baton and running with those they spiritually parent, all while leaving a legacy of love.

As you read this book, you will see how legacy kept them focused on the big picture and concentrating on the long-term building of a structure that would ensure the life of the generations to come.

As Christians, we are admonished to consider the godly examples found in the previous generation. Hebrews 13:7 says, *"Remember those who led you, who spoke the word of God to you; and considering the result of their conduct, imitate their faith."* We all need a place of belonging, a place to be nurtured and loved, a place where we are given strength and encouragement to grow and become the person God created us to be. From the beginning of time, God's place was (and still is) the family. Let's make it our personal goal to create longevity of life in the Spirit for our children—natural and spiritual—not just leaving an inheritance, but also building a lasting legacy.

In this book, you will clearly see and discern the difference between an inheritance and a legacy. The inheritance of our father can be spent in a moment's time, but legacy is for eternity. This is a must-read book for anyone who wants to leave a legacy!

Building together with Him and you,
John P. Kelly
International Convenor,
ICAL (International Coalition of Apostolic Leaders)

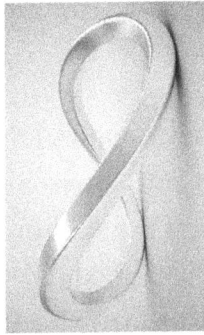

Foreword by Bishop Bill Hamon

Dr. Moyer has blessed the Body of Christ with some vital truths for the generations. The Scriptures forcefully direct us to leave a legacy to our generations that follow us. I have believed and practiced these truths for my sixty-seven years of ministry. All three of my children have followed my wife and me in being Christians in ministry leadership. My eleven grandchildren are all serving the Lord, and they are raising my twenty great-grandchildren to serve the Lord Jesus. God gave me a ministry with a special anointing for reproducing like kind, and we have trained over half a million saints in the prophetic ministry.

Dr. Moyer's book will help you leave a legacy to your children and also to those whom God gives you to disciple into their calling and destiny. This book should be read and practiced by every Christian who wants to leave a legacy to those over whom they have an influence.

God bless you, Dr. Moyer, for having the father heart of God and the vision to leave a legacy of wisdom and truth for those who desire to fulfill the Scriptures for reproducing, imparting, and disciplining your own family and the family of God.

Thank you, Dr. Moyer, for you have expressed my heart and passion, which is like yours for our generation and for generations to come.

Bishop Bill Hamon
Christian International Apostolic-Global Network
Author of 14 books on Church Restoration and
raising up the Joshua Generation.

Dedication

Proverbs 13:22

> *A good man leaves an inheritance for his children's children, but a sinner's wealth is stored up for the righteous.*

I would like to dedicate this book,
The Art Of Legacy,
Living on After You're Gone

First, to our children:

- Melissa Moyer
- Russell S. Moyer, 3rd
- Marissa Chisholm Kaus
- Dallas Chisholm
- Jon Moyer, our nephew

To our eleven grandchildren:

- The late James Russell Moyer
- Corianne Moyer Nelk
- Deborah Moyer

- Samantha Moyer
- Ayla Chisholm Kaus
- Carter Chisholm Kaus
- Max Kaus
- Rebecca Kaus
- Natalie Chisholm
- Nashville Chisholm
- Nova Chisholm

To our great-granddaughter:
- Ava Washington Moyer

And to all of our spiritual sons and daughters, with special recognition for these who have faithfully co-labored with us at Eagle Worldwide Ministries, Canada.

- Alex and Patty Wallace
- Miguel and Laura Simon
- Derek and Joanna Adams
- John and Victoria Irving
- Reid and Victoria Grassick
- Joe and Denise Zivanovich
- Ashley Almas

Acknowledgments

I would like to acknowledge all the mentors, teachers and coaches in my life:

- The late Anthony Chiccino
- David Gey
- Pastor Paul Wetzel
- The Late Ruth Ward Heflin
- Rev. Joan Gieson
- Dr. Jane Lowder
- Apostle John Kelly
- Bishop Bill Hamon

For help and support in finishing this book, I would like to thank Harold McDougal, my publisher, Kelty Barber for proofing and editing and Linda Cove for the book cover design.

I must also acknowledge my wonderful wife, life mate and parenting partner, Mave Moyer. who has co-labored with me in this incredible harvest season.

Endorsements for
The Art of Legacy

"Eight years ago I was ordained and set into the ministry God had for me by Dr. Russ Moyer. That day God introduced me to my spiritual father, and I will forever be grateful for him. It is God's will that fathers leave an inheritance to their children. It is true in the natural, but also in the spiritual. *The Art of Legacy* is all about that. This book is a prophetic download from the heart of God into the heart of Dr. Russ Moyer.

"Not only do we learn about the importance of legacy and what it is, but Dr. Russ also gives us a road map with all the indicator posts so that we, too, can do it. It is indeed an art to leave a legacy, and Dr. Russ developed that art in his walk with God. He models in his daily life exactly what he shares here in the book.

"This is a book for everyone, and it could not have been written at a more critical time. In it, you will learn about God's heart for all of us. It is about discipleship, mentoring, raising up sons and daughters, learning how to walk and work together in relationship and community and fellowship like a real family should."

Marlene Bilodeau, Senior Pastor
Refuge Under His Wings, Quebec, Canada

"Do you want to leave a legacy? *The Art of Legacy* is a practical handbook for establishing legacy in your own life and ministry.

"We have been mentored and raised in ministry by Dr. Russ Moyer, and have walked alongside him since 2001, leaning on, gleaning from, and building on the ministry foundation he has established over the past twenty years at Eagle Worldwide Ministries.

"Dr. Russ practices what he preaches. Not only does he write about bearing fruit, impacting our world and affecting future generations, but we have seen firsthand how he lives it, breathes it, teaches it and imparts it.

"It is very evident in his life, in our lives, and in the lives of all his sons and daughters that Dr. Russ is indeed establishing a legacy, one that we are very proud to continue.

"We pray this book will encourage you to create a legacy of your own, one that will live on after you're gone!"

Victoria and Reid Grassick
Eagle Worldwide Ministries

℘

"Dr. Russ Moyer is a true spiritual father, mentor and pioneer in the faith. As spiritual children of his for nearly twenty years, we have been immensely blessed. He lives what he preaches and truly has a heart to see the next generation raised up to continue advancing the Kingdom of God.

"Under Dr. Russ's leadership and guidance, we have experienced so much growth as ministers. We now pastor one of his churches and are so grateful for the way he has poured into us, trained us and activated us, launching us into our destinies. He saw value within us that we didn't recognize in ourselves and, like a true father, nurtured our giftings and helped us become the ministers we are today.

"*The Art of Legacy* is a true representation of Dr. Russ Moyer's heart for the upcoming generations and the future Body of Christ. Leaving a flourishing legacy and helping others reach their fullest potential is a selfless, beautiful act, and for the way he has done that for us, we will be forever grateful."

Derek and Joanna Adams, Senior Pastors
Eagles' Nest Fellowship
Ancaster, Ontario, Canada

"By most historic accounts, Jesus was crucified around 33 AD. He started His ministry at age 30, so in just a few years He laid out not only what was relevant for His generation, but also that which would continue to change the world nearly two thousand years later. How did He do that? By making disciples who were cultivated, equipped and prepared to carry on after His ascension.

"*The Art of Legacy* is not only an excellent commentary on New Testament principles but fresh revelation proven through the experience of Dr. Russ Moyer, who is a church planter, ministry builder, business leader, life changer and nation shaker. In this book, he gives us a treasure of knowledge so that we might not only see success now, but also leave the next generation a legacy."

Glenn Garland
Ashland, Virginia

✆

"*The Art of Legacy* is a book birthed from a life that understands that God is a generational God. As I read this book, I felt the passion of Dr.

Russ Moyer's heart to see the next generation equipped, loved and flowing in their gifts. This book will inspire you to examine your priorities and life and make any necessary changes, to build a legacy that will last for generations."

Elizabeth Tiam-Fook
Founder, International Young Prophets
Santa Rosa Beach, Florida

❦

"*The Art of Legacy* is a must read for anyone who has a heart to produce fruit and fruit that will last! From the heart of a natural and spiritual father, Dr. Russ imparts practical wisdom with engaging examples that will both inspire and challenge you.

"I have had the awesome privilege of walking with Dr. Russ and Pastor Mave for seventeen years as a spiritual daughter and living with them for over eight. They sacrificially live the principles in this book, modeled after the life of Jesus, that have so powerfully touched my life and the lives of countless others. Whether you are passing the torch or receiving the torch, God will use this book to change your life and cause you to be fruitful beyond your dreams. Get ready to live your destiny and leave a legacy!"

Patty Wallace
Pastor, The Revival Centre
Hamilton, Ontario, Canada
Vice President of Administration
Eagle Worldwide Ministries

ɶ

"When Russ Moyer began his ministry now many years ago, he very quickly realized that what he was dealing with was not just personal—his own spiritual well-being and his own gifts and callings. His concern was to be much broader: the well-being and development of the whole family of God. He not only counted it a privilege to be able to bring sons and daughters into the Kingdom; he cared about those sons and daughters and wanted to see them do well, grow and expand into the fullness of their calling. This led him to consciously give them opportunity for growth.

"It was not enough that he prophesy; Dr. Russ wanted his sons and daughters to prophesy too.

It was not enough that he learned the secrets of prosperity; he wanted them to prosper too. The result is that now, many years later, Russ Moyer is not a one-man show. He never was. His vision has turned into the company of evangelists, apostles, prophets, pastors and teachers who are part of Eagle Worldwide Ministries.

"And now, Russ has done the Church world-wide the great favor of putting the secrets of his successful body ministry into a new book, one that he has aptly entitled *The Art of Legacy*. It is unique, timely and powerful."

Harold McDougal
McDougal & Associates

&

"He is the God of Abraham, Isaac and Jacob. He is a God of the generations. David had his Solomon, Elijah had his Elisha, Paul had his Timothy, and we remember their work and ministry because of their successors, because they left a legacy.

In today's world, many hold tightly to what they have because they are afraid if they share it, it will be taken away from them, or another person may do it better. Jesus said, *"Unless a grain of wheat falls into the earth and dies, it remains alone; but if it dies, it bears much fruit"* (John 12:24, ESV). This is legacy, dying to self to produce lasting fruit through sons and daughters.

Russ Moyer does not speak as one who has studied this topic; he speaks as one who has lived it. I am the fruit of his passion for fatherhood, having been mentored and raised up in my gifting and callings that he saw in me before I knew I had them. That is what a spiritual father does. That is what legacy is.

In this book, you will learn the secrets of the lost art of legacy and the practical steps to apply them to your own life so that you, too, can walk in them and start leaving a lasting legacy.

Miguel Simon
Vice President of IT, Media and Web Development
Eagle Worldwide Ministries

℘

"I have had the honor and privilege of walking with Dr. Russ Moyer for over twenty years. He has poured his time and life into Victoria and me. He is a father to us in the faith. We can never thank him enough for what he has sown into our lives and ministry.

"In his new book, *The Art of Legacy*, Dr. Russ Moyer has captured the heart of God. Russ views the Christian life as a relay race, passing the baton to each successive generation. We have a lack of true spiritual fathers in the church and so many people are crying out to be mentored, to be fathered. This book will challenge you to leave a spiritual legacy in the lives of this younger generation.

"Myles Munroe, a powerful father and author expressed legacy like this: 'True leaders don't invest in buildings; they invest in people. Jesus never built a building. Why? Because success without a successor is failure. So your legacy should not be in buildings, programs or projects; your legacy must be in people.'

"Like Dr. Russ, I encourage young people to pray for a spirit of sonship. Pray for fathers to help you grow and reach your God-appointed destiny."

Pastor John Irving
The Gathering Place of All Nations
Aurora , Ontario, Canada

My friend, Dr. Russ Moyer, has written a very important and timely book. *The Art of Legacy* is a prophetic book that makes the connection, building a bridge, between where we stand now and where God is leading His people in the future. Legacy is key for longevity.

Several years ago the Lord began speaking to Janet and myself about the significance of legacy, so much so, that we even gave our second daughter that name. Read this book and discover for yourself the reason why *The Art of Legacy* is so vital in this hour.

Joshua Mills
Bestselling author, Moving in Glory Realms
www.joshuamills.com

Contents

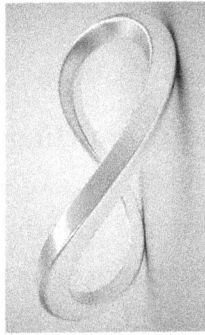

Preface by Mave Moyer

Ministry is a sacred trust between God, the leaders of the ministry and those who follow us *"as [we] follow Christ."* These precious people have been entrusted to us by the Lord, and we are responsible to teach them the truth of the Word of God, keep them safe and help them to fully receive His transformational power. Ministry is not a "right"; it's a privilege. Paul showed by example his accountability to the council in Jerusalem, and we must do the same.

I don't know why so many "think" or "feel" there is no need for accountability today. We need accountability more than ever before. God uses divine alignment to protect us as we answer our call, but many in ministry today are rebellious and detached from any relationship that includes correction and accountability. They make decisions independent of any oversight and end up hurting themselves and those who follow them. Accountability and spiritual alignment are wonderful things. They help to shape and sharpen us and will keep us from error as we yield and listen to those God has brought into our lives as a point of wisdom and safety. Accountability and alignment are biblical concepts and are much needed in the Body today. This is what will produce true sons and daughters.

Could it be that we are not where we need to be spiritually because we are not rightly connected and aligned to the people who can help us reach our full potential? God has a purpose and plan in spiritual family alignment, the same way He had a plan for our growth and success in the natural family setting. Ruth needed Naomi to reach her destiny, Timothy needed Paul, and Elisha needed Elijah. True alignment is not about a person controlling us; it's about having a more seasoned spiritual "parental figure" in our life to provide loving encouragement and wise counsel.

A true parental influence wants us to succeed above and beyond. He or she is a mentor who can see and stir up the God-given gifts, talents and potential on the inside of us, so that we might be established in the ministry we are called to. We all say, "Jesus is Lord and King," implying authority and obedience, yet we fail to align ourselves with His Word when it comes to being in right spiritual relationship with others. We all love Jesus as Savior, but what about as "Lord"? If He truly is our Lord, then that requires something of us. It confronts our independence and tendency to be "on our own" and calls us to be accountable to the Word of God and to one another, that we might become mature in Christ.

The Word of God is relevant to every culture and every situation. Everything in the world around us may change, but the standard of the Gospel will never change because God, who put it in place, never changes. It's time to get into God's ordained relational alignment for our divine assignment and bear fruit that lasts for the Kingdom of our God.

Mave Moyer

A good man leaves
an inheritance to
his children's children,
But the wealth of the sinner
is stored up for the righteous.
Proverbs 13:22, NKJV

Introduction

Over the last four or five years, the message outlined in this book has been burning on my heart, and I am convinced that it's on God's heart too. You and I must leave a legacy when we leave this earth. What is legacy all about? It's about bearing fruit and fruit that lasts. It's about impacting our world and leaving it in a better state than when we came into it. This means that we must positively affect the next and younger generations.

This should not be a problem, for our God is a generational God. He is the God of all seasons, the God of every season—personal, business, ministry and professional. He is not just the God of one group or the God of one age. He is God of all, and His life is for all generations.

On our prophetic journey to destiny we pass through many periods. For those of us who are getting up in years, we must now focus and finish on legacy. We must have legacy as our mindset, legacy as our motive and legacy as our method

In my own journey, there have been many different seasons. To live by the Spirit and be led by the Spirit we must truly recognize our season and the seasons in the heart of God and allow Him to lead us prophetically—faith to faith, glory to glory, and season to season. We must continue to keep our hearts open to change, transition and transformation.

The one thing that is very constant in every season is change. From the moment God touched me, He has been ministering change to me from Romans 12:1-2:

> *Therefore, I urge you, brothers and sisters, in view of God's mercy, to offer your bodies as a living sacrifice, holy and pleasing to God—this is your true and proper worship. Do not conform to the pattern of this world, but be transformed by the renewing of your mind. Then you will be able to test and approve what God's will is—his good, pleasing and perfect will.* NIV

Everything about my life has been related to the life cycle of the eagle, which biblically, naturally and prophetically has been woven into my spirit, my walk and my journey. The eagle is the prophetic symbol for the office gift of the prophet and the gift of prophecy, and God has graced my life with this gift.

As good as life has been, there comes a time for all of us to depart from this earth. My recent bouts with cancer have forced me to consider this truth more seriously than ever before. The way I see it, there comes a time for each of us to pass the baton to the next runner. This Christian life is not a sprint, and it's not a marathon. It's a relay race, with other runners involved. Just as with the passing of the baton in a relay race, the successful and timely transference of power and authority is essential if we are to finish well. This means that team-building and recruiting must be an integral part of our everyday work. Fatherhood, discipleship and mentoring must be given ample time.

Jesus was our example, and He successfully passed His ministry to men and women He personally had mentored and prepared. Successful Christian leadership involves influence and delegation. Responsibility without authority and correction without relationship only breed rebellion. But I can only lead those who desire to follow, and so we need to pray for a new wave of sonship to strike the Church today.

Many have failed to successfully hand off the baton of ministry because they could not let go. To them, letting go meant giving up. Could the next runner possibly do as well? But we must give the next generation a chance to prove themselves. Someone gave us a chance. If God did it for us, He will do it for the next generation too. He is the God of Abraham, He is the God of Isaac, and He is the God of Jacob.

Yes, there may be problems with our next and younger generations. Some may not have been properly parented or prepared, and may be struggling with an identity crisis. We must find ways to overcome these situations, restoring family and paternity into the lives of our sons and daughters.

Every encounter in every season and phase of this journey has given me a fresh revelation of another dimension of the heart of God and His love for me. He is teaching me continually how to give love to Him and receive love from Him and how to give and receive love from my brothers and sisters, sons and daughters, friends, neighbors and, yes, even my enemies. God is always pressing me on toward a deeper place in the destiny call, to fulfill His two greatest commandments:

> *Then one of them, which was a lawyer, asked him a question, tempting him, and saying, Master, which is the great commandment in the law? Jesus said unto him, Thou shalt love the Lord thy God with all thy heart, and with all thy soul, and with all thy mind. This is the first and great commandment. And the second is like unto it, Thou shalt love thy neighbour as thyself. On these two commandments hang all the law and the prophets.* Matthew 22:35-40

In the process of fulfilling these two commandments, we all have to learn to deal with relationship issues and negative emotions like betrayal, offence, love, hate, anger, rage, depression and trauma that come to all of us.

The ultimate truth about legacy is that there can be no success without a successor. Are you working to pass on your faith, your gifts and your ministry to succeeding generations? Are you ensuring that you will live on after you're gone? That is *The Art of Legacy*.   *Russ Moyer*

                                        The U.S. and Canada

JUST AS WITH THE PASSING OF THE BATON IN A RELAY RACE, THE SUCCESSFUL AND TIMELY TRANSFERENCE OF POWER AND AUTHORITY IS ESSENTIAL IF WE ARE TO FINISH WELL!

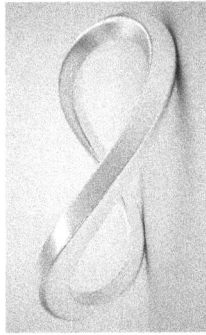

Chapter 1

Turning Hearts

See, I will send the prophet Elijah to you before that great and dreadful day of the LORD comes. He will turn the hearts of the parents to their children, and the hearts of the children to their parents; or else I will come and strike the land with total destruction. Malachi 4:5-6

As I noted in the introduction, for the past few years there is something that has really been on my heart, and I believe it is also on the heart of God. That is the next generation. What God is doing right now is bringing the hearts of the fathers back to the children and the hearts of the children back to their fathers. He is recreating a family model that He established long ago but that was somehow lost along the way. This is vitally important because of what is happening in our modern society.

God's heart is broken today because of the brokenness of families. In the natural, we are in a season of ministering to a fatherless generation, a generation that has experienced dysfunctional family relationships. There is a hunger and a thirst in the hearts of this generation for true family—both in the natural and in the Spirit. I am convinced that the local church is the family model that God intends to set in place, and it is time that we began to experience this restoration of the spiritual family.

To me, the most important thing about ministry is not having good meetings, exciting services or even wonderful worship. That is all very important. But the most important thing is discipleship and mentoring, raising up sons and daughters, learning how to walk and work together in relationship and community and fellowship, like a real family should.

The Great Commission of Jesus to His Church is: *"Go therefore and make disciples of all the nations, baptizing them in the name of the Father and of the Son and of the Holy Spirit, teaching them to observe all things that I have commanded you; and lo, I am with you always, even to the end of the age.* Amen!" (Matthew 28:19-20, NKJV). Yes, discipling and training those who come into the Kingdom of God as new babes is God's plan for duplication and multiplication, and it is His spiritual family model.

I am convinced that this is the missing link in our society, and until we get it right in the Body of Christ, society doesn't have a chance.

This year we in Eagle Worldwide Ministries are celebrating twenty years of ministry in Canada, and many from our first traveling ministry team are still involved in the ministry today. I remember with fondness the days when we gathered the first small group of young people in the back room of our old farmhouse. That was our first congregation, a youth group. Those were awesome days!

As God raised up those young people, we did many things together. We went to Rochester, New York and ministered to the underprivileged, serving and helping to feed the hungry at the Rochester Urban Center. We set up a platform on Ontario Beach and ministered to many teenagers and young adults we met there.

Our young Canadian team prophesied over individuals, over cities and over nations. It was their first ministry/mission experience. We took them to the city below Rochester, and there we ministered to the homeless and led many to the Lord.

In 2002, Mave and I were married, and many wonderful things began to happen.

A Catholic priest, Father Stan, called me from Vancouver, British Columbia. He had been referred to me by a call worker at Crossroads Center. He said, "I was told you were an exorcist."

"Something tells me you're Catholic," I said.

He told me his story of difficult health issues and addictive behavior and the fact that he had only recently been released from the hospital. He wanted me to minister deliverance to him over the phone, but I told him I would need him to visit us so that we could minister to him in person.

When he said he couldn't come because he didn't have any money to travel, I answered him, "If this is God's will, then He will provide," and then I prophesied over him that his bishop would pay for the cost of his travel.

He thought that was very unlikely, but I said, "Well, I'm a believer."

He called me two days later and said, "You'll never believe what happened! I met with my bishop, and he is going to pay for my ticket to Toronto."

I asked him when he planned to arrive and he said, "I'll be there tomorrow afternoon."

I picked him up at the airport and took him to our home, the little farmhouse. There we ministered deliverance and inner healing to him, and the Lord gloriously set him free. He was also baptized in the Holy Spirit and began to receive dreams and visions. Gold dust began appearing over both of us. It was an amazing moment—in his life and in mine. Somehow there was an immediate bond between us.

Father Stan went back to Vancouver Island and rejoiced with his bishop about his freedom and then called me about two weeks later. He said he had decided to take a sabbatical and come and live with Mave and me and travel with us and the rest of the team in ministry. He came and lived and traveled with us for about nine months.

At the same time, we also had a couple of missionaries from the U.S. staying with us, and our home was also our office. We did the bookkeeping at the kitchen table. Our family room was turned into our prayer room, and we took a large closet on the first floor and turned it into my private office. We also had three desks in the living room. Whatever you do, don't despise small beginnings.

In this way, our team became a close-knit family of spiritual sons and daughters from all different backgrounds and spiritual expressions. This was all a totally foreign experience to me because I had been a wealthy businessman for more than twenty years, had lived in a 7,500 square-foot house on twenty acres of land, with security gates and an 1,800-foot driveway. Needless to say, I was accustomed to having my privacy and my luxuries, but God knew best. In those meager, close quarters, we became family, a real spiritual family. God re-taught me, re-parenting me Himself and turning me into a father in the Spirit. I am so grateful.

God was setting the tone for how our ministry was to go forward into the future. Those were not just any young people; they were our very sons and daughters in God. Later, as God began to establish this ministry, He brought us young people from the Brownsville Revival School of Ministry I had attended in Pensacola, Florida, and they also became sons and daughters in ministry.

We built our base on those who were willing to walk with us in faith, and that has been an extremely wonderful thing for us throughout these years. God has gathered spiritual children around us, and they have been willing to walk together with us by faith to see God's plan and purposes fulfilled—for Canada, for the U.S., for Israel and for the nations. Our spiritual children have understood the mission and mandate of God and been willing to sacrifice to see it come to pass.

Now we are in our season of legacy, and whatever legacy we leave will live on after we are gone. Many of our spiritual children have now become pastors and leaders in Eagle Worldwide Ministries, many are part of our core leadership team. They have taken over administration operations, media, accounting, outreach ministries, and our network of ministries. It has been such an honor to see what the Lord has done in their lives, as they have been raised up in their calling and gifting and set in their places of leadership in Eagle Worldwide. They now stand ready for Mave and me to pass the baton to them.

When I first went to Canada to preach the Gospel, there was not much talk of discipleship and the mentoring of sons and daughters. There were not many prophetic voices in the land. I, too, had not had a great deal of prophetic training because that had not been the nature of ministry in the past. There were prophets, and they prophesied, but they seemed to blow in and then quickly blow out again. And it all seemed so mystical.

But the revelation that God gave me, when he launched me out in the year 2000, was about making sons and daughters and about discipleship and mentoring, and I have been doing that ever since. The groups that gathered around us had received, until then, very little spiritual parenting. But I began to gather them, teaching them and mentoring them individually about their gifts, about how real those gifts were and how they worked. I taught them that they were all called to ministry, and then I taught them to work together as a team. I taught them that our work was not just as a church; we were called to extend and advance the Kingdom of God on every side.

Now, after twenty years, our earliest sons and daughters are in their forties, fifties and early sixties, and they continue to serve the

Lord faithfully. Those who came up to Canada from Pensacola were then in their twenties and thirties. They are now in their forties and fifties, but we continue to add many young people to our number. We love to spend time with the International Young Prophets group. This is the next generation that is coming up, and to see the fire of God they have and the hunger in their hearts is very exciting for me.

It's all about the revelation that God gave us many years ago, that we were living in the days of Elijah. We sang that song everywhere we went. The cry on my heart was repentance, turning back to God, the purity of the Word of God and signs and wonders accompanying that Word given to us by God's Spirit. This was quite different from the typical church ministry.

Our main thrust was based on this passage from Malachi:

> *See, I will send the prophet Elijah to you before that great and dreadful day of the LORD comes. He will turn the hearts of the parents to their children, and the hearts of the children to their parents; or else I will come and strike the land with total destruction.* Malachi 4:5-6

43

I sensed that it was important for us to come into right alignment so that the blessing of God could come into the earth. The next fresh fire would once again be released, that very fire of Pentecost and the power of God and the signs and wonders that happened in the Acts of the Apostles. We were convinced that God was the same yesterday, today and forever, and He began to knit together the family that now makes up Eagle Worldwide Ministries.

Among us, there is a broad base of giftings and callings. We have fivefold ministers who have launched out as missionaries, pastors, evangelists and prophetic voices. We have marketplace leaders. In fact, we have a whole network of ministers and ministries. We have outreaches that feed the hungry. Each of our spiritual children has taken the gift of God and the call of God and walked it out in their own way.

It has been the greatest blessing in my life to see these men and women become who God called them to be, not just to come to church and sit to be entertained, but to be equipped and empowered and then launched into their destiny. To me, that is the development of legacy, and I believe it's the true ministry of Christ on the earth today.

One afternoon, as I was flying into Pensacola, I feel asleep on the plane and had a dream. I saw a tree in the middle of our sanctuary, and it was laden down with fruit. The most incredible thing about the tree, however, was that every branch bore a different type of fruit. There were peaches, and there were cherries; there were apples, and there were pears; and it was all coming from the same tree. The Lord was speaking to me about the supernatural way He was supplying a variety of gifts and callings to the members of His Body. He was showing us our children, all from different branches and all bearing different fruit, but all from the same tree. Each of them is able to produce the very fruit that is most needed at the time for whoever comes to eat of that tree. What a miracle this is!

It was an amazing picture for me to see. It demonstrated that as we have embraced the gifts of God in each other, encouraged those gifts in one another and celebrated the gifts in one another, God has caused a tree to come forth as a ministry to many. The branches of that tree signified and symbolized our spiritual children bearing their gifts and callings that God has placed in them, and each of the branches represented a supply for someone's need. I believe that's what we're supposed to be doing in ministry today. We are to bear fruit and fruit that lasts. That is to be the legacy of any ministry and of every individual who walks in that ministry.

Ministry is not just a thing; it's about people, people who are involved in blessing others. The Church is not just some inanimate object; we are the Church. The Church is made up of people, and every single one of them has an important part to play. We must celebrate the uniqueness and the value that is to be found in each person individually and what they bring to the table, what they have to offer the rest of us.

Whether we like it or not, we're in the people business, and we must be ready, willing and able at all times to meet the needs of those whom God sends across our path. That's what ministry is all about. We're not in this for the income; we're in it for the outcome. That's what our Kingsway Ministry is all about. That's what our outreach ministries are all about. That's what our traveling ministries are all about.

That's what our Apostolic Resource Centre is all about. We are equipping the saints for the work of ministry, so that we can be mobilized in the earth, not just as the family of God, but as the army of God, to fight the necessary battles, win the wars and see victory in each person's life.

I have been so blessed with the success stories we hear coming forth from those who work with our Kingsway Ministry. People are being delivered from every kind of addiction and are now faithfully serving God and walking out their life in His Word. Lives are being changed, radically turned around, and some of those formerly broken people are coming into ministry.

Many people have been hurt by the church, but that is not to say that the church is a bad place. You can get hurt anywhere. When you interact with people, wherever it may be, there is the chance that you will be hurt. You can be hurt at your neighborhood Walmart. Church is a place we can go to be healed—if every member will work together and do what they're called to do. I have so loved that supernatural tree, symbol of our working together. That is a legacy that will live on after we're gone.

The home is often a place of deep hurt and relationship problems. When people are more intimate, they have the capacity to hurt each other more. But that's just part of relationships. You can expect to have greater victories, but you can also expect to experience moments of despair and discouragement because of hurting one another. The closer you are to someone, the more difficult it is to maintain a healthy and proper relationship.

Mave and I are both middle children from large, dysfunctional families. We were both part of blended families before blended families were normal. When I was in school, I was one of the few children who lived in a blended family situation caused by divorce. Today, this is quite common, as more and more children are affected by the breakdown of the family. There is also the fact that neither parent is now at home during the day. Both are working and have busy schedules because of the financial pressures of our modern society.

The predominance of social media is another factor that works against this new generation. It plays such a great part in their lives and often not a healthy or helpful one. For sure, it has a negative effect on them developing good, healthy family relationships. Twenty-first-century children are suffering from the lack of this important dynamic. They often don't have the right kind of person to speak into their life and guide them as needed.

God was very gracious to me to send some wonderful people early on in my Christian walk. I got saved in my mid- to late twenties. But I was quite stubborn—Italian, outgoing and strong. You know how we are at that age. I wanted to serve God, but I wanted to do it my way. I had my own way of thinking about how to do things. I really didn't have the spirit of sonship. I was impatient—impatient with my parents' generation, impatient to make my mark. The result was that I would have to make a lot of mistakes and learn everything the hard way.

Then, after a time, I suddenly began to see the negative cycle that I was in, the roller-coaster ride of being up one day and down the next. I would take a few steps forward and then a few backward. I now realized that I needed to change my thinking, and I needed input from other people who were more experienced, more mature and had more wisdom than I had.

This came to me so strongly that I began to cry out for a spirit of sonship to come upon me. I could have the greatest mentor, friend or parent, but if I didn't listen to them and change my ways, I was headed for a fall. I could have the best people speaking into my life, but if I didn't have a spirit of sonship that caused me to receive what they were saying, it would do me no good.

Dysfunction had its roots in the Garden of Eden. Dysfunction is the fruit of disobedience. Everything that God had made was perfect, but after the fall of man, we can see the family already beginning to fall apart. God had created Adam and Eve and brought them together to show a true understanding of how wonderful family can be. But they messed it up, and from that moment, it didn't work like God had intended. And, since then, things have only gotten worse.

Eventually, when God looked down, He didn't like what He saw. So, He opened the heavens and sent rain. It rained and rained until the earth was flooded and much of mankind was drowned. Then, however, after the flood was over, Noah and his family quickly fell back into their old habits and into family dysfunction. Men were selfish and looked out for themselves so that the next generations had no one to look to for guidance.

I believe that Malachi 4:5-6 is where we are on the timetable of God. Finally, after so many years of family dysfunction, we are seeing a shift that is turning back the hearts of the children to their fathers and the hearts of the fathers to their children.

I am a father, and I know how challenging raising a child can be these days. Being a parent is a hard job. In one way, it's a life sentence (I say that in a positive way). Once a father, we are always a father. I love my natural children, and I love my spiritual children, but both of these arenas are challenging.

In some ways, spiritual parenting is even harder than natural parenting. You want to give your children the right guidance and care, but you also have to keep your distance in certain areas of their life. You cannot control others or make every decision for them. You must respect them and the gift of God in them enough to believe that they will hear from God for themselves and be able to move in His purposes and plans. As a spiritual mom or dad, that's always a challenge. However, we can know our children by the Spirit and then hold them at arm's length, letting them find their own way, trusting God and each other.

With others (Mave includes herself in this category), it's more challenging to raise natural children. Because they are your own flesh, you feel like you have more of a stake in the matter and should be able to tell them what to do, and they should listen. This, of course, is crazy because when our children come to the age of accountability, we have to be able to let them go and let God do in their lives what He needs to do. He is God, and we are not God. God had a lot of work to do on Mave in this regard.

Mave got saved when she was fifteen, but she didn't start serving God then. It was more than fifteen years later that she began to hear Him speak to her, and she responded. That incorruptible seed had been planted in her, and it eventually bore fruit. She knows that many of those same seeds were planted in her children through the years, and she has the confidence that those seeds, too, will bear their fruit. But she has sometimes struggled to trust God with those natural children.

As for Mave's spiritual offspring, they are all serving God and are happy to serve Him. It amazes her that they are still as much on fire today as they were when she first met them years ago. The same can be said for all of the sons and daughters that came out of Pensacola. They are always on fire for God and always on fire for His service, always busy about the work of God. God has already preordained these things for us to walk in.

I will never forget the day that Reid Grassick heard God speak to him. Victoria, his wife, was with me in the office, and we were just having a regular office day. Then Reid called. They were living in Watertown at the time, and he was out in the yard doing some yard work when God spoke to him and said, "You don't need to do all this work because you're not staying here." They had just bought that house and hadn't lived in it even a year. This was the beginning of a progression that moved Reid and Victoria closer to the purposes and plans of God. His ears were opened to hear what the Spirit of the Lord was saying, and before long, they were set in place to oversee our campground in Copetown, Ontario. Being able to witness this experience in my spiritual children was amazing.

Reid had been working in a factory. He was the foreman on his job and had always been a leader in business, but now God was putting him into the Father's business and would train him in a whole new way on how to deal with new things, new people and new places. Eventually, the two of them also began to pastor a church. It is amazing to see how God works in their lives, to bring them to the place where they need to be. I am believing that He will do exactly this same thing in the lives of all our children—both natural and spiritual.

In the coming chapters, I will share more about legacy, about developing sons and daughters, about raising up the next generation and I'll give you some examples of how that works. God is looking for sons and daughters with a servant's heart, and as we yield our hearts to the Holy Spirit, He'll make us more like Jesus, who came to serve and not be served. This is *The Art of Legacy*.

GOD IS BRINGING THE HEARTS OF THE FATHERS BACK TO THE CHILDREN AND THE CHILDREN TO THEIR FATHERS, RECREATING A FAMILY MODEL THAT HE ESTABLISHED LONG AGO!

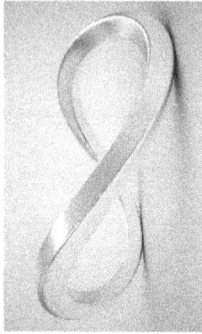

Chapter 2

Living On After You're Gone

A good person leaves an inheritance for their children's children,
but a sinner's wealth is stored up for the righteous.   Proverbs 13:22, NIV

We are good and honorable spiritual parents when our goal is to create longevity and legacy for our children, both natural and spiritual. We may not have experienced this personally growing up, but I know God intended for us to have a hope and a future and to succeed. And His will is for us to help facilitate the same in the lives of our children. Through our legacy, we can live on because of the life we have lived in the here and now.

Not long ago, I talked this scripture over with a friend of mine. She had the understanding that this was all about money. I told her that if we can firmly establish a legacy of spiritual heritage in the lives of our children, we have set them firmly on a path for success in every regard. Legacy keeps us focused on the big picture. It keeps us concentrating on the long term and gives us a structure that ensures the life of generations to come. That's what I want for my children—both natural and spiritual. I want them to be dependent upon God, not dependent upon what I might leave them or what I might have stored up for them. They will need to be dependent upon what God is able to supply for them from day to day.

Mave and I have traveled in ministry now for the last twenty years, and God has established a great work through Eagle Worldwide Ministries. It has been a journey of faith, and we have always depended upon and trusted in God to supply our every need according to His riches in glory, not according to how many meetings we could do or any kind of side work we could get. We have trusted God, and my desire is that my children— both natural and spiritual—would be focused on the fact that God is their Supplier. If I can get them to focus on that truth—that He is able—they will always have more than enough to do every good work God has called them to do.

I fully agree with that scripture and the way it is written, and I certainly want to leave an inheritance for my children. To me, wealth is wealth. It's not just money. Wealth includes wisdom and strength and understanding and love and hope. It includes all the good things you can receive from the Father.

My dad left me an inheritance of sorts, but it had nothing to do with money. When my mother died, Dad had to sell his small row house because of what he still owed on it and move into an apartment with my youngest brother. I had gained some early parenting experience helping to raise my two youngest brothers from babies while my mother worked third shift in an asbestos mill. Unfortunately, she died of cancer related to the asbestos that got into her lungs, went up her spine and caused a tumor on the brain. She was only forty-three. Dad, more than fifteen years older than Mom, was devastated by the loss. I then had to step in and help with my two brothers again.

At the same time, I was raising two children of my own and helping with my brother Gene's son, Jon (first, when he was just a baby and then, again, when he was in his late teens). Consequently, Jon is like a son to me. He moved to Pensacola with his family, lives very close to us now, and is a big help and support to us personally, as well as being involved with our church here—The Dwelling Place.

Dad was a tough man, a truck driver for thirty-seven years. He had been a boxer and a gambler when he was younger and a high diver at the Steel Pier in Atlantic City when he first got out of the Navy after World War II. He didn't have much money, but the inheritance he left me included an understanding of people—street smarts and common sense. One of seventeen children, Dad only had a seventh-grade education, and he loved me the only way he knew how.

The only discipline Dad understood was corporal punishment. I didn't have a fear of the Lord growing up, but the fear of my father kept me from prison and a much more troubled life. He loved and fathered me the same way he had been loved and fathered himself.

For many years, Dad's harsh discipline caused me to carry some real hurt in my heart and gave me a perverted view of what the love of Father God was like. When I eventually got saved and started to deal with those feelings and emotions (with God's help), I was not only able to forgive my father, but also to receive and understand the love he had given me. I realized that I had respected him as well as feared him, and now I truly appreciate the inheritance he left me.

I had the honor of leading Dad to the Lord near the end of his life, and I look forward to seeing him again in Glory! My sister and I had to help pay off his small debts and expenses at his death, but he left us much more.

The only monetary inheritance I ever received was $300.00 from my grandmother. I went out and bought a stereo set with it, and for many years, every time I listened to that stereo set, I remembered her and my grandfather and my Italian roots and heritage.

We think way too much about money. I was driven by it for many years, chasing success and running away from poverty, only to realize that success and the world's riches was a formidable foe to my soul and my spiritual well-being.

Success is not about fortune and fame, and neither is legacy. It's all about the intangible things that are poured into us by others of influence. These would include coaches, teachers, mentors, family and friends. The things they teach us develop character, integrity, wisdom, faith and heartfelt healthy relationships, along with memories and personal experiences we can tap into in the various seasons of life. These things, along with education, no one can take from us. They are ours. That is our true and lasting inheritance, and that's the kind of legacy I want to leave.

What kind of person you are and how you function around other people is much more important. Are you leaving a mark that makes a difference in the hearts and lives of others? If not, what mark are you leaving? Is what you are leaving of more value than a mere coin? Who you are should be impacting all those around you. Are you leaving part of yourself with others?

When you met someone, walked with them and worked with them or lived with them for a season, were they left changed? Leaving nothing but dollars and cents, cars and trucks or properties of some kind is fine and good, but that's here today and gone tomorrow. The legacy I'm talking about will last forever.

While here on earth, have you spoken of things that are important? Did you dwell on things that make a difference long term, things of the heart? When push comes to shove and you are looking down the barrel of a gun, these things suddenly come into focus. I know what it is to be financially wealthy, to be successful in business, in sports and in the media and now also in ministry. But when my moment of truth came, none of that mattered to me. Suddenly, I had to ask myself, "Have I made a difference in the life of the people I have come in contact with? Can I say that I can leave this place better than I found it, leave that person richer in their heart, their mind and their spirit? Did I encourage them? Did I strengthen them? Did I empower them? Did I say the right things at the right time? All of this is so much more important than the natural things I might leave behind.

Unfortunately, too often children look to the possibility of a natural inheritance that can, in some way, make their life easier or more profitable. But it is actually the spiritual and emotional inheritances, the impact that your mother or father had on your life, that is of far greater consequence. That is the real inheritance. What you have gathered from this inheritance becomes who you are and what wisdom you have in life. If it is good, then gold and silver will follow.

Part of the problem is how we determine success. What is success? Is it money in the bank or cars in the garage? Or does it consist of things like determination, truth and honesty, loyalty, faithfulness, knowledge and wisdom. These are the things that bear fruit and bring wealth, wealth that lasts. All the rest is wonderful and can be very important, but not the most important.

Poverty is certainly not the answer. The answer is found in education. I speak of education in a general sense, teaching and training that breaks the cycle of ignorance in our lives, letting us know something about others and about how to walk with them and work with them.

The humblest of people can learn from every experience, from every relationship and from every encounter. I am learning every single day and am more able to take in knowledge today than I was twenty-five years ago. It is because my mind, in this season, is so open to listen and to learn from the life experiences of others.

The things of which I speak are eternal. Money and personal possessions, material things, are here today and gone tomorrow. It is the things of the heart that are eternal. The love that we share with each other is eternal.

When Jesus came to Earth, His whole purpose was to destroy the works of the enemy in our lives and to produce the love of God that's been shed abroad in our hearts by His Spirit. If we can impart that love to our spiritual children, as well as to our natural children, we will see them walking in a place of success.

As parents, whether we know it or not, we're always building a legacy and, at the same time, building a better life for those who come after us. When we first started in ministry, we were pressing in every day to God by faith, for our rent, for our gas, for our car, for money to get to the next meeting. Today we no longer need to press in for those small things, but now we're pressing in for the larger things that God is doing in our realm of influence. Our former young people, who are now in their forties, are still pressing in to God for those things with us. That will be our legacy.

Legacy is about equipping and helping others to become, first, what God intended them to be and, then, to invest in them the call, the vision and the mandate of God. He has a mandate for certain regions of the earth, and we have many friends in ministry who raise up spiritual children and some who don't. We've been involved with ministries that never gave a thought to legacy or succession, and they are now dead in the water, having had no one to carry them forward. This has always been our heart, that whatever we establish here will be carried even further by our sons and daughters. We want them to go to a higher place in God and to do greater things in Him.

Our greatest desire is to be better parents than we ever imagined we could be. Spiritual parents leave a legacy and have a plan of succession. I am so thrilled that we are now walking in a place of legacy and that we have our succession plan in place. Our intention is to run hard and finish our race alongside of those who are in line to take our place. That is not a wish for our work to die in the water, but, rather, that it would arise out of the wave of God's Spirit into an even higher place.

Eagle Worldwide Ministries is not about you and me. It's about all those who come together to facilitate God's purpose and plan today in their respective regions. Whether we are in Canada or the U.S. (or in Heaven), our desire is that our spiritual children will continue to shine on and move forward, that they will continue to press in to God by faith, knowing that He is their Provider, that He is Jehovah-Jireh, that He will provide all their needs according to His riches in glory, not according to what we can do for them or what we can help them with. Each one of us must look to God because, in all truth and honesty, when push comes to shove, the legacy we have created is in the heart of God. He will place that in the heart of our children, and they will continue to move and flow by the power of His Spirit to see it come to pass. To me, this is what legacy is all about.

We have been to nearly two hundred churches across North America and around the world, and as I travel, I get the opportunity to meet people who have done great works for God, building wonderful ministries, churches or networks of ministries. But as I talk to them about this matter of legacy and transition, I find that my thoughts are not particularly well received. When I speak to an elderly person who has been plowing for a long time, ministry has become their life, and they are happy doing it, what I have to say suddenly speaks to them about their humanity, their mortality and something that, all too often, has been left undone—preparing for the end.

Every man or woman who has ever lived on the face of the earth had a beginning and an end, and we all have to face that fact. We have been given a certain season in which to work for God, but eventually our season will end. Our end, however, is never God's end. For Him, it is just a beginning. But it is a very different season, a new season, with opportunities for new people to shine. Will your sons and daughters be among those who lead this next generation?

The thought of legacy seems to frighten many. We each go from season to season and glory to glory, but eventually we all end up in the grave. That should not be a frightening thought. The question is: what have we left behind that will continue to speak? Was it all about us? Or did we build a family that continues to do the work once we have passed on?

Far too many people have not done a very good job at establishing a legacy. It's almost as if they feel like they are giving in to death if they prepare for the inevitable. The gift of fatherhood is one of the greatest gifts God has given us, and we have the privilege, not only of working for God here and now, but also of preparing future generations for what they will face when we are gone.

It has been my sad experience to help some ministers close down their very fine works because they had not raised up anyone to take their place. They had not trained those whom they had raised up, equipping and empowering them. They had not imparted a vision to the next generation for that work.

Today God is speaking to many about the future, a future without them, and He is showing them the right time and the right way to put in place those who will carry on their work after they have gone on. God is presenting us a model for establishing legacy and transition in apostolic and prophetic ministries.

If we walk in the Spirit, these things should not overtake us by surprise, but too often that is exactly what happens with Spirit-filled ministries. God is showing us new models for marketplace ministries, and He is developing a New Testament model all over again, so that His people can see it and experience it. It's one thing to hear me share about it or to read what I have to say about it, but many of us need to see it to properly understand it. A picture is worth a thousand words; people need to see it modeled, put into action.

Most of my family, including myself and my brothers, developed ADD and ADHD. As noted, I helped raise my two youngest brothers. Gene had trouble focusing and sitting still. As a consequence, he didn't work very well when manuals were required. But, if he saw something, he could do it. That was just the way it was. When you see it, you, too, can do it. We need to model legacy so that the rest of the Church can see it in action and then produce it in deeds.

What we see is worth so much more than what somebody has spoken. That's why we have to begin to model or demonstrate what legacy is all about, what Body ministry is, what spiritual parenting is. God is showing us what healthy family relationships are like in the Church and what husbands and wives walking together in ministry and covenant relationship can do. He is establishing models in every area. And you and I must begin to model legacy so that others can see it and learn. They will not be able to do it just because they hear you say it.

Some may say, "I've heard a lot that I know to be true, but I can't envision it. Once I see someone else walking it out, then I will be able to do it too." That's why we need to model it for others. We believe that we are in the end times, and God is transitioning us into an end-time army, an end-time family. Now we must prepare to pass the baton to the next generation so that we can walk this thing out together. We will do it by living and walking, working, relating to one another, learning and gaining from each other's experiences—with all of our victories and defeats.

We must be able to speak into each other's lives at different times, and this only comes from an open place of legitimate relationship. That's why Christianity and our walk is not about religion; it's about real relationship.

One great thing about legacy is that through it we can outlive our earthly life. Every life will leave some sort of legacy, but what will your legacy be? Each of us must decide. Dying or not dying is not an option we have. Leaving a legacy or not leaving a legacy is not an option. The question is: what will your legacy be?

The legacy we leave will be the life the next generations live. We will leave a legacy, but we get to decide what that legacy will be. That may well determine the course of future generations. The more we can pour into this generation, the more we can love them and lead them in a place of understanding and grace, the more we can set them up for success.

When we came into ministry and were pressed on every side, we resorted to great times of intercession and prayer, and God gave us strategies and filled us with understanding, opening up for us realms of possibilities and revealing to us what He wanted us to do. As we stepped out into that revelation, an amazing thing happened. God began to put this ministry together. It happened through dreams and visions, through times of deep intercession, and through times of waiting on God's Spirit.

In those hours in His presence, He birthed the future of this ministry in our hearts and showed us the spiritual children He would gather around us, children of the same DNA, and now they are walking out the vision and already creating a legacy for the next generation.

Pastors are amazing and wonderful, and we all need them in our life. They do a great job. However, they have far too long been the person in the church that people look to for everything. That was never God's intention. His intention was that there would be a parental aspect in the house, a pastoral team, that would serve as spiritual parents to the entire family of God, but that there would also be sons and daughters who would rise up and do the work of ministry in the same way.

When we have kids in the house, someone has to do the dishes. Someone has to take out the trash on Saturday morning. Someone has to cut the grass. Someone has to clean the bathrooms. We all have chores in the house of God, and God set that model in place for the Body, that every member would work together to do what God has called us all to do, to facilitate the ministry in the house.

All of our combined efforts are for those who need healing, those who need a word of hope, those who need encouragement, those who are struggling in their relationships, those who are struggling to pay their bills and have enough to survive. Families who have lost a loved one need our help. Men and women who are bound by addictions and could be living on the streets need us all to work together for their deliverance. We must be those who are ready, willing and able to facilitate the ministry. This is the present-day ministry of Jesus through the Body of Christ, His family. He has set in place, not just an operating model of the family of God, but one that is willing to move in succession and legacy, so that you and I might outlive our lives through the legacy plan of God. That is *The Art of Legacy.*

Now, before we close this chapter, I want to pray a Father's blessing over you right now:

Heavenly father,

I put Your name on Your children, and I ask You, Lord, that Your love, Your hope,

Your favor, Your strength and Your wisdom would begin to rain down on the hearts of those who are reading this by faith. I pray that they would find their right place, their right relationship, and that You would connect them heart to heart and spirit to spirit in perfect alignment with the spiritual family that You have established for them, that You would guide them, protect them, bless them and prosper them in all that they do.

Let the covenant blessings of Abraham and every other covenant overtake them now, overtake them wherever they go, in whatever they do, and let Your light shine in and through them, that Your favor shine, and Your blessing overtake them.

In Jesus' name,
Amen!

LEGACY KEEPS US FOCUSED ON THE BIG PICTURE. IT KEEPS US CONCENTRATING ON THE LONG TERM AND GIVES US A STRUCTURE THAT ENSURES THE LIFE OF GENERATIONS TO COME!

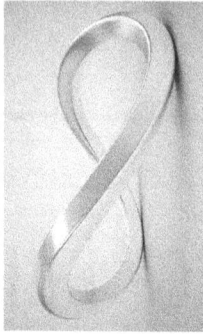

Chapter 3

Building Bridges to the New and Next Generation

Now therefore give not your daughters unto their [the heathen's] sons, neither take their daughters unto your sons, nor seek their peace or their wealth for ever: that ye may be strong, and eat the good of the land, and leave it for an inheritance to your children for ever.   Ezra 9:12

I am very excited about the new thing God is doing all over the earth. He is raising up a new breed of leader, a whole new generation. And many new things are happening. Yes, Jesus is the same yesterday, today forever, but right now He is singing a new song, and He is doing a new thing. I want to kiss what He's kissing and do what He's doing.

I am very excited about the new generation coming up and their leaders and what's on their hearts and the prophetic side of what's happening right now in the Kingdom of God. It is awesome. God loves every generation.

It's exciting to see what God is doing and how things are changing. There are changes and shifts that are taking place just about everywhere in every stream. A fresh wind is blowing, and that is wonderful to hear. But are we actually listening?

I don't just want to hear this new generation; I want to listen to what God is saying to them and through them, and I want to adjust my thinking and my heart to what God is doing in their hearts because they're the generation that's coming up behind us to accept the baton. The question is: how do we bridge the gap to the next generation? From what I've seen, I have an idea of what they are doing through social media and their own lines of communication, but I want to understand more. I want to understand them.

It's interesting. Right now, there are actually five generations alive at once. We have those born before 1944. They are in their seventies now, and many of them are going on to be with the Lord. Many in that generation were founders of great works. Many of the ministries they founded are still in operation today. The Baby Boomers fall into that category. Most of them are now between the ages of fifty-five and seventy-five.

Personally, I am seventy as this book goes to press, but I'm not ashamed to tell people my age. People are looking for someone they can trust, someone who has experience, someone who has been where they want to go. Sadly, we don't have many mentors these days, especially in the church, people we know and love and can trust and look to for guidance. That is the real calling of a spiritual father. We even need spiritual grandfathers to lead us today. Baby Boomers are generally considered to be those who were born from 1946 to 1964.

Then we have the GenXers (1965-1979). GenXers are in their forties and fifties now and just entering into some of the best years of their productivity. They have paid a price to get to this place in life and ministry. Some haven't made it to this point, having been knocked down by some social situation or other along the way. Today's generations, however, are facing issues the older generations never dreamed of (like the epidemic of internet pornography and the pandemic, when the whole world as we know it, is shut down and will be forever changed).

This is the generation, the GenXers, who are actually now in their leadership prime. They've had life experiences and a chance to prove some of the principles of life and have some success. The folly of youth is now behind them, and they are prepared to lead. I see the mantle of leadership upon them.

The next generation, the Millennials or Generation Y (1980-2000), digital natives, are out of university now and starting their lives in the workplace. Far too many of them are faithless, claiming no religion at all. If you ask them if they are a Christian, they will answer as if you had said, "Are you an American?" Those who make it through college have been so bombarded over the years with neo-liberalism and secular humanism that they are the same as atheists.

They are "practical atheists" because they don't believe in the sovereignty of God or that He actually affects our circumstances. Even if they know *about* God, many of them don't know God.

Then we have Generation Z, the New Silent Generation (born 2000 and later). Some of them have graduated from high school, but many of them are still in high school and even middle school and grade school. This generation spends an inordinate amount of time on Snapchat, Instagram, Facebook and other social media platforms.

Other generations did this sparingly, but not the GenZers. They live and function on social media, sending photos back and forth with their "friends." When you see them in a public or group setting, they often ignore each other and pay more attention to their devices than they do the relational encounter of the moment. Those real-life encounters actually take them out of their comfort zone and into the real world. This makes their online "friendships" seem very strange to the older generations. You have to wonder if they are having any real and meaningful conversations.

It seems to us, in the older generations, that what young people are doing today with their snapshots on Snapchat, etc. is not developing any very deep relationships. Are they dealing with real people or just snapshots of life? We need to see that person in the context of their life, not just a moment. Who are they? Can I feel them now? A snapshot of a person is not who that person really is. Can this lead to any real communication or meaningful relationship? It seems to work for the younger generations, even though the rest of us are left scratching our heads.

This generation is connected digitally, but are they connected personally and relationally? We, of the older generations, would go out together for a cup of coffee and have a deep conversation, but this new generation doesn't seem to have a lot of that type of opportunity. When they are together at a gathering of some sort, a party, for instance, they don't seem to talk to each other much. Each one keeps glancing at their phone to see what new snapshot is available. In our view, this is a complete social disconnect. This allows them to remain safe, in a form of fantasy world, avoiding reality and real-life issues.

Here is where the Church must step in. In the church, we can experience real community. The church is a place where people can interact in many ways and experience true fellowship.

Unfortunately, many churches have responded to this younger generation in what I consider to be the absolutely worst possible way. Because recent generations seem to have a more limited attention span, churches have opted to shorten their services, use more video presentations, musical specials instead of heart-to-heart talks. This is missing the point and just feeding into the lack that already exists. This generation needs real connection, and they don't know how to find it.

In the areas of communication, marketing, and promotion, everything is changing. It is now a high-tech, high-speed world, and many of us in the older generations don't understand it very well. The best we can do sometimes is to withhold criticism and quietly observe the shift taking place. What is needed is a bridge between generations and not a wall of criticism.

Just as in any family, we have people of all ages, experiences and opinions. It has always been the responsibility of the older generations to nurture, train and equip the younger ones coming up. This doesn't mean that we have to fully understand each other. It does mean, however, that we must respect each other and work together for the good of all concerned.

It reminds me a lot of a game that was played as we were growing up. It was called Double Dutch, and it consisted of two jump ropes going at the same time. The two ropes were going in opposite directions, and the person who dared to jump into the middle of them had to time it precisely and then move quickly to jump each of the two ropes without being snared by either. As children, that looked like so much fun to us, and we wanted to get in on the action so badly, but how to do it was another thing entirely. If we were encouraged that we could do it and given the opportunity, we loved it. If not, we somehow felt deprived. Now is the time to push aside the insecurity and jump in between the generational differences.

This, I feel, is what the older generations are now facing. We want to get into the digital game, and we are watching others play it, hoping to see an entry point, but too often we are left frustrated because we don't understand how to do it. The younger generations just laugh at us. It all seems so easy to them, just common sense. To them, it is intuitive. This has left generations without a bridge to unite them and may be why so many young people are leaving the faith. It no longer seems relevant to their daily lives. For our part, we still want to play the game and are eager for someone to show us how. Don't leave us outside as spectators to your world. We want to get into the game, too.

Far too many of our older generations have written the newer generations off. Because we can't understand their world, we no longer want to be involved with them, and we just let them go their own way. But our generations have also seen great change. In our lifetimes, we went from a horse and buggy society and a farming culture to living in modern cities, driving cars, flying across country and around the world in jet airplanes. And we adjusted to all of that just fine. Why, then, can we not participate and keep up in the digital virtual age? Would we prefer to go back to dial telephones and walking to school every day?

The world is clearly not going back, and neither am I, so we must adapt to the new and help every generation make the best of it. Far too many Boomers don't want anything to do with modern society, but modern inventions are just one more way for us to spread the glorious Gospel of Jesus Christ to the ends of the earth. I am falling in love with change.

We didn't despise radio when it came along. We didn't reject television when it became popular in our time. We didn't refuse to use telephones when they became available to us. And yet they all represented huge generational shifts. Instead of refusing them, we adapted to them and their potential to reach more souls. Therefore, we cannot afford to reject this digital virtual age and its utterly amazing potential. Technology represents a way to reach the largest number of people in the shortest time, and that's what the Gospel is all about.

The latest talk is of 5G networks that will be even faster, more wide-reaching and more adaptable to new uses. So we must use social media and all other new outlets to do what we are called to do. Instead of writing off the younger generations, we must love them, recognize their unique calling and work with them to accomplish what we cannot do without them. Their day is coming, and we must prepare them for it.

In recent years, I have personally experienced some severe health issues, and that has caused me to be more concerned than ever for the next generations. In my own life, things are changing. I have a fresh vision for the future and can see that it's not all about me. If I can come forth with a fresh message, that's great, but my primary concern is for the coming generations. My cry to God these days is, "How can we empower this next generation? How can my life experiences help them to grow and learn so as not to make the same mistakes I made?"

They won't have to climb the same mountains because we have cut a tunnel through them. They won't have to cross that same river with all of its dangerous rapids because we have built a bridge to the other side. How can I continue to impact this generation?

I certainly want to bring forth a pure Gospel message for the next generations, but I want to do more than that. I want to be there for them. I want to set an example for them and then teach them all that I can possibly teach them. More than anything, I want to empower them and prepare them for their own lives and ministries.

I had the privilege of attending Bible school in Brownsville, Florida, and there, in the midst of revival, I learned a lot. However, there was much that I did *not* learn, and I came away from there with some misconceptions about ministry. Some of the practical side of birthing a work and building that work were never covered in our studies. Therefore, when I launched out on my own into Canada, I had no idea what I was about to face. I would like for the generation that is now launching out to know more and be better prepared for what is ahead. When they hit a snag, I want them to know that it's not a dead end, merely a detour, a challenge that must be faced and overcome.

People who have been serving the Lord for decades have a wealth of information, a wealth of wisdom and revelation knowledge that needs to be passed on to the next generations. When we speak, it is not just throwing out some new ideas. We have been there and done that. We have faced some giants and overcome. We have seen both hard times and good times and know that God is always faithful.

Keeping up with the latest generations seems futile at times, and we are tempted to think it's not worth it. But they need us just as much as we need them, and we need them just as much as they need us. God set solitary people into families for a reason. Each member contributes something important to the whole, and without each individual, the family cannot make the same impact.

All too often, young people resent their elders until they have matured some themselves, and then they realize how much they owe to those who loved them and sought to guide and form them ... even while they were not being very cooperative. We must take the long view, knowing how important the task of parenting is and what the fruit of it will be in the end.

Usually, if we love someone, care about their opinion and believe in their future, they will eventually realize this and be grateful. That they are sometimes temporarily ungrateful and even resentful should never discourage us. We must be mature enough to know our task and the importance of it, and people's opinions, even sons and daughters, should never matter that much to us.

If we are dealing with a natural child, we often have more patience with them. Can we not accept every soul placed in our care as our child? Who gave birth to them is not the important part. What their destiny is and how we can help them reach it is the most important thing.

When the next generation looks at you, what do they see? Do they see a hypocrite? Do they see someone who loves them as they are? Do they see someone who believes in their future?

It is not unusual for older people to be totally perplexed about the priorities of the newer generations. For instance, the next generations seem to be all about appearance. They put a lot of store in how they look. If we reject them because of that, we may miss out on the opportunity to become mentors to them.

I believe that I have been inspired by God's Spirit to speak out on these issues because you may be at the right place at the right time and in the right season of your life to become a bridge between generations. If you are old enough, experienced enough and mature enough to have something to offer to the young people of our day, and you are also mature enough and experienced enough so that older believers will be able to trust you and work with you, you may be an answer to prayer. Get ready to build that much-needed bridge.

When I look at young people today, I try to remember what I was like at their age. Like many of them, I thought I knew everything, and I thought I had everything I needed to win the world for Jesus. I was very optimistic.

These new generations grew up with participation trophies, meaning that everyone who participated got a trophy. We had to earn our way while theirs was seemingly given to them. But human nature has not changed all that much. Paul wrote:

> *Do you not know that those who run in a race all run, but one receives the prize? Run in such a way that you may obtain it.*
>
> 1 Corinthians 9:24, NKJV

The new Dr. Spock mentality for raising children has sometimes robbed them of a key element of life. At times, in the context of church, we will say, "We don't want to compete, we want to complete." However, there is a healthy competition in life in which we learn to keep our eyes on the prize and run the race to win. Let us motivate this next generation because they are ordained and destined for victory.

But it's not only in the winning that our character is molded; it's also in learning how to experience defeat. Learning how to lose graciously and how to get back up and get back in the ring develops the perseverance necessary to be a champion.

If the new generations can recognize that they need the wisdom of their spiritual fathers and mothers, grandfathers and grandmothers, they can quickly learn and grow and be blessed.

The younger generations need to be able to trust us, but we also need to be able to trust them. They need to be able to demonstrate to us the integrity needed for the job, but they are looking to us to see if we demonstrate to them that same integrity. It works both ways. The old and the new need each other, and their future depends on each other.

As many American children grew up, they became what has come to be called "latchkey children." When they got home from school, there was no one to greet them, no one to see that they did their chores, completed their homework, behaved themselves properly and kept out of trouble. The testimonies of that group of people were very powerful. What children now go through as they grow up cannot be compared to this. There can be no doubt that today's generations desperately need parenting. The problem is: will they open their hearts to a parent figure? They definitely need spiritual fathers and mothers, but will they trust one? This is our challenge. Unless the younger generations see in us the pure love of God, they will not follow either our example or our teachings.

Relationship forges the way to real influence in their lives. Many have been hurt by poor or absentee parenting. So that they will have true influence in their lives, we will have to re-establish the foundation of trust.

The apostle Paul wrote:

> *Be ye followers of me, even as I also am of Christ.*   1 Corinthians 11:1

The New King James Version renders this as:

> *Imitate me, just as I also imitate Christ.*

If you are just as broken and messed up as everyone else, who do you expect to follow you or listen to your advice, especially in a spiritual sense? We need someone who can be trusted across generations. Therefore, you need to be an example of what it means to be godly husbands and wives, fathers and mothers, brothers and sisters. Let us set the example for others to follow. Model the Christian life for all to see.

There are many who talk about what needs to be done, but, as the old saying goes, "Talk is cheap." What we need today are more people of action, who, by their example, empower future generations to do what needs to be done by showing them what to do and how to do it.

The great thing about the apostolic and prophetic, is that the Ephesians 4 model was designed to equip the people of God, the saints for the work of the ministry:

> *... for the equipping of the saints for the work of ministry, for the edifying of the body of Christ.*
> Ephesians 4:12

What are we equipping them for? For what God has called them to do. In large part, this cannot be done by immature and inexperienced people. Therefore, it must be the rallying cry of the older generations. It is no longer about just building our ministry. Hopefully, we have something built by now. Now it is time to dedicate our energies to preparing the next generations. During this last season of your life, concentrate on pouring into them. We cannot do this without purposing to do it, without working at it. It doesn't just happen. Give yourself to this very important discussion, this timely moment taking place throughout the Body of Christ.

As we shift into this new season, let us all have raised levels of expectation of the great move of the Spirit of God to come and the subsequent blending of the generations. This will require much dialogue, and that requires relationship and giving those to come something to think about and emulate. It's time for these discussions to come to the forefront. This is *The Art of Legacy*.

WHAT IS NEEDED IS A BRIDGE BETWEEN GENERATIONS AND NOT A WALL OF CRITICISM! LET US MOTIVATE THIS NEXT GENERATION BECAUSE THEY ARE ORDAINED, DESTINED FOR VICTORY!

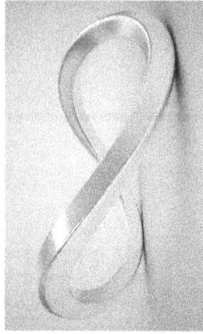

Chapter 4

Bridging the Gap

And God said moreover unto Moses, Thus shalt thou say unto the children of Israel, the LORD God of your fathers, the God of Abraham, the God of Isaac, and the God of Jacob, hath sent me unto you: this is my name for ever, and this is my memorial unto all generations.

Exodus 3:15

There is nothing quite like the blending of the generations. Elderly people can do some things that young people cannot, and young people can do things that the elderly cannot. When the two are brought together, with all of the ages in between, it becomes something very powerful indeed.

One of the things young people are better at than us is reaching people outside of the church—athletes, for example. We need both the work outside the church and the work inside the church, utilizing media and social media, such as entertainers, athletes, politicians and connecting and communicating on Facebook, Instagram, Snapshot and Twitter, etc. Each age group seems to have its own favorite way of communicating and reaching people who wouldn't necessarily hear a spiritual, Christian-oriented message or attend church.

Young people are often more adept at moving in different environments, and that is important. We need a breakdown of the church walls so that we can reach those who are without. Let us, therefore, walk together in unity and understanding.

As I am writing this book, we are currently in a new season of reset, change and transition, during the pandemic lockdown, so that we are unable to gather together in our church buildings. Social media has become paramount, the only way we can continue to have church. So, through necessity, the Lord has been able to bring forth change and realignment. The walls are down, and the harvest is here, there and everywhere. We are touching people we could never have reached in the confines of a traditional church. So even this, which the enemy meant for evil, the Lord has turned around for our good and His glory.

Developing trust among the generations is one of the most important things we need to be doing these days. That trust will come when we have an understanding of proper relationship. Then we can dialogue back and forth between the generations and become relevant to one another.

I thank God for the privilege of working with young people through the years, and I thank Him for the young people who have chosen to work with us. I often enjoy throwing a ball into the air to see what they will do with it. To me, it is delightful and often surprising to see what they come up with. They, too, feel the need for bridging the generational gap.

Young people are tired of pretense and are looking for an authentic move of God. They're looking for how they can touch God for themselves and how they can practically see Him moving in their own daily lives. Some have grown up going to church, and some haven't had that benefit. In both cases, they are looking for the supernatural power of God that we have consistently confessed is available but that really hasn't been seen much in the last twenty years or so.

Young people are not just looking for the authentic power of God; they're looking for the authentic power of God moving in people's lives, transforming them and making them new.

Many young people no longer identify themselves as Christians. They may call themselves Christian, but they are actually identifying with their parents' faith, even though they are often not very familiar with it. It is surprising how many in this generation did not go to Sunday School and haven't read the Bible. So, they don't have an understanding of what they really believe in or have any true faith of their own. To them, Christianity and religion are negative terms, having become tainted and powerless.

What does it mean to be a Christian? It does *not* mean belonging to a certain church or living by a certain set of rules. It means being followers of Christ, and it means that He is our example. There are so many voices calling out to us today, wanting us to follow their example, but when we follow Christ, we can be sure that we're on the right track. We need to have a personal relationship with Jesus and follow His principles.

Young people look to heroes, and Jesus is a superhero. They are interested in power, and He is the superpower. He is the higher power. They are looking for love, and He *is* love. His love is transformational. If you want to look for a reformer, look to Jesus. He was a radical revolutionary whose presence in the earth brought total reform.

The power of Jesus' love can totally transform you—and not just the way you think. When your mind is renewed, then your whole being can be renewed. The things you say and do will be renewed as well. Scientists have proven that our mental health is much better when we become men and women who practice our faith.

The many demands of modern life can tax your strength and spirit. We have many personal responsibilities, and when we put on top of that our ministry responsibilities, it can become overwhelming. This makes the church culture, the family of God, so much more important. You have brothers and sisters in the Lord who are always cheering you on. If and when you need them, they are there for you. They can be someone you can talk with and with whom you have things in common. This alone proves very healthy because it enables you to keep your mindset in the right place.

Therefore, being authentic, being honest in your relationships with one another, being transparent with each generation is so important. Young people today expect transparency. They want to see the real you and the real me. And the only way you can be your true real self is through the power of Jesus. Being transparent and real will enable us to build bridges between generations.

Jesus loved children, and they were important to Him. He said that we need to come to Him as little children, for He loves child-like faith. He taught His disciples not to hinder the children from coming to Him because the Kingdom of Heaven belongs to them (see Matthew 19:14).

People who understand and express true love also love children, love young people, love young adults, love adults and love the elderly. All of these ages have their purpose and are ordered by God Himself. They are all essential. No one in the Body of Christ is without merit or purpose, and we must learn to work with all and learn to respect all. However, it should be clear to all of us that the younger generations need our attention. Then again, the older generations need our attention as well. In fact, in working with and relating to that older generation (the young at heart), our affirmation and attention helps them to feel like they still matter.

We all need to feel like we're important to God, and we are. Our older natural and spiritual family members need our attention in a very different way, especially toward the end of their lives. They still have something to give, but they also need to receive from us. They also need love and affirmation.

Being able to relate to all generations is so important, and part of that is knowing who you are dealing with. What are their individual needs? You can't expect nearly as much from a child as you can from someone older. Why? They simply don't have the experience or even the mental capacity to make the right decisions. They need a lot of teaching, and this requires a lot of love. Just like the rest of us, they are looking for love, and they are looking for someone to follow, someone to emulate.

Bridging the Gap

When you are in a worship service, the most important thing for you to do is worship so that the younger generations can see what worship is all about. Show the younger generations how to entertain the Spirit of God instead of having to be entertained, and they will soon be emulating you because that's what children do. Young people want to know that you love them and care about how their day goes, that they are not just a number to you.

It is amazing what you can glean from the younger generations. Why amazing? Older people have had years to learn and more experiences to learn from, and so you expect it from them. But children are so innocent and so trusting that they will say things that absolutely blow you away.

Young and old alike have things to share. If you have only seen someone sitting on a church pew, you may not realize what they have to offer, but when you start talking to them and develop a relationship with them, you suddenly begin to see the depths of their wisdom. Very often older individuals have lived a life that was not at all easy. In the process, they learned many things.

Sometimes we feel that the younger generations have had life relatively easy. They had no wars during their growing-up years, and their families were not thrown into serious economic depression. They were not forced to learn the dignity of hard work, but had things given to them. That developed a different mindset. Can you see why these two generations would not be able to easily understand each other? If the two generations never take time to converse, how will each one know what the other one has to offer? However, every generation has its moment of challenge, trial and tribulation. Every generation has something to share and something to bring to the table.

Some understand what it's like not to know if there will be food on the table tomorrow or not, and others have no clue about how that would feel. Some remember having to turn the lights off at a certain time to avoid being bombed. Others could never understand those feelings. There are great gaps between generations that need to be bridged. It is amazing how simply talking with the other generations helps us to understand each other.

People who have never lost a spouse could not possibly know what that feels like. It is considered by many to be one of life's greatest challenges. The older generations married young and stayed together a lifetime. They can hardly remember what it was like to live alone. Therefore, when they lose their spouse, it is an earth-shattering experience. You have to learn to meet people where they currently are in life and understand them through those experiences.

The simple art of listening to one another is so much a part all of this. Each generation has somehow believed that they knew everything, and none of us do. We all have a lot to learn, and we can learn from one another. You have a lot to share with those who are under you (age wise or experience wise), and you have a lot to learn from those who are over you in the same sense of the word.

Education and learning experience is a life-long quest. We learn from others and from our own personal experiences, as well as from the educational system. We need to have an open mind and an attitude of humility that allows us to learn and receive from one another.

It is hard to imagine what some generations have been through, but to insist on always being the one sharing and failing to receive from others is just as great a mistake. Take time to hear from others, giving them the opportunity to share their heart with you. Don't insist on doing all the talking. That is part of what young people resent about older generations. We like to monopolize the conversation.

If I am constantly talking about what I've been going through, then it's very hard for me to hear what you've been going through. Quiet yourself sometimes and hear what others have to say. How else can you come to an agreement?

It is so important to identify generational differences. Those young people who refuse to identify themselves as Christians obviously think the church has an image problem. So we need to work on that. Too often the younger generations see the church as being too judgmental or even hypocritical, far too political and not nearly loving enough. If that is our reputation, then we've earned it.

For those who grew up during the years of the televangelist scandals, hypocrisy is what they saw. It didn't help that they were exposed to the grunge rock and gangster rap environments. The proponents of gangster rap were trying to describe life as it was on the streets of our cities.

The group known as Nirvana with Kurt Cobain was very influential. Cobain later took his own life and two other band members were killed. This left a lot of cynicism, doubt and mistrust among their followers. Young people must overcome their cynicism and learn to trust older generations.

This type of cynicism can actually be passed down from one generation to another. The hope and truth of the Gospel is the antidote to cynicism and deception.

When we talk about discipleship, it has to encompass much more than just making sure a person is truly redeemed. They also need to be set free from all forms of generational influence, becoming hopeful and willing to listen to the perspective of older generations, trusting them and giving them a place to speak into their life. At the same time, we need to be careful not to squash the dreams, the ambitions and the perspective of a generation that's coming up. They'll get to know sooner or later how tough things are. We want to be realistic, yet positive and encouraging, bringing a balanced and uplifting message of hope.

If the parents of a young generation coming up were not active in church life, then the children also have a tendency to be turned off by church. "I'm not very religious," some say, "but I *am* spiritual." Whereas *religion* used to be a good term, being religious today is definitely a negative. There has been a redefinition of some terms. This "bugs" some in the older generations, but it need not. As words are redefined, stop using them in the same way. Learn to operate in the current environment. Such things are not worth fighting over.

Something you hear a lot these days is this: "Well, I don't have to go to church to be saved. We are the church." It's true; we are the church, but the Bible is very clear about the importance of gathering believers together.

We gather for many reasons—to worship, to pray, to hear from God, to learn, and to fellowship. Many of us would not be able to learn about God without the special atmosphere of the church.

If the younger generations are looking for family relationships, the church is where to find them. When God established His Church, He made it a family, His family. The pastors He set over the Church were to be pastoral, but they were also to be parental. Their authority was to be exercised with the love of a father. Pastors are to facilitate the ministry of the whole family, not just a chosen few.

In our work with the young prophets, we often have opportunity to hear the heart of the younger generations, and what they are telling us is that they want and need family in the House of God. They know better than anyone else that they sometimes don't know how to act properly. How could they? We all had to learn. They need (and want) parental advice in these areas.

This is unusual because, in the natural, this is just what many young people are trying to get away from. They have not understood the discipline their earthly parents tried to impose upon them and often resented it and rebelled against it. They want to honor leadership and be respectful, but they need coaching. They need parenting, and they need love and encouragement.

It all comes down to being transformed by the washing of the water of the Word in our own minds and having our mind renewed. What I think (my opinion of things) is not necessarily what I should be taking hold of in this hour. I should be seeking to know and understand what the Word of God has to say about any given subject, and I should seek to operate in His Word. There is power in the Word, but I can't operate in the Word if I haven't taken that Word in. God's Word is the blueprint for successful Christian living; it is *His* blueprint for successful Christian living. We must all come back to the place where the Word of God is our standard, and I am often amazed and disappointed when I find that many don't want to do that today.

When anyone looks at our lifestyles as believers, they should see the Spirit of God, the life of God, the love of God and the abundance of life that Jesus talked about.

It all boils down to our personal choices. I can get up in the morning and tell myself how tired I am, how much I have to do, and this and that, or I can be the best prophet in my own life, speaking life to myself and others. I can set my day in place, calling my morning into being and can have authority over the day. When I live my life in this way, that's the greatest example to anyone we are attempting to parent, mentor or discipline.

We must be authentic, real and sincere, being who we are. It's understandable that the younger generations would be cynical when they see hypocrisy and a lack of authenticity in the church today. Let's model the real.

Again, whatever we do, we must be authentic, not putting on airs, but being who we are. There is much cynicism among the younger generations because of the lack of authenticity in the church today.

Another problem that is affecting the younger generations is that we have created structures in which people have very little time for fellowship with each other. It's as if we are all punching a time clock, in and out, and there is no time to get to know each other. This is not a healthy family environment, not a good place for all to grow and develop. Recognizing this, we must create space for conversation, relationship and fellowship.

In a family, every member is important and each one has something to contribute. It is important to recognize what each one brings to the table. Each person must become comfortable in their particular role, and whatever we have to do to make that happen must be done. Let's challenge ourselves to rise higher, to change. God promised:

The Art of Legacy

The glory of this latter house shall be greater than of the former, saith the LORD of hosts: and in this place will I give peace, saith the LORD of hosts. Haggai 2:9

The idea that something greater is coming is not always pleasant to the older generations, but that doesn't mean that God loves us any less. If the latter is to be greater than the former, then we have a duty to pour into the rising generations to prepare them for what is to come.

Parents are often neglectful of their children because they feel that what they have to do is more important than spending time with children. But unless we pour into coming generations, how can we be ready for the greater glory that is to come?

Too many of us are focused on "my ministry," "my career" and "my life," when the most important aspect of our ministry is passing the blessings of God on to new generations. There must be a cultivation of every generation, or the entire family of God, the Church, will suffer.

I preach a lot on family, and I like to create a family atmosphere in the church so that people of every age and every level of maturity can feel welcome and blessed. I want all ages to feel that they are in a safe place and that they can tell me what they need so that I can help them become who they were intended to be. As moms and dads in the Spirit, we must give every generation the time they need to glean from us, and our doors must always be open to them.

There is way too much selfishness in our society today, and this has bled over into the Church. People in their forties and fifties need to grow up, put away their cynicism and frustration and quickly step into a place of leadership in the Church family. They need to realize that leading is first by example. They should honor the generations ahead of them and glean from them while they still can. They will very soon be inheriting much of what the older generations are and have, and they need to know how to handle wisely the things being handed down to them. This is a great honor, and they must show that they are up to the task.

At the same time, they need to become mentors for those under them, setting godly examples. Again, some of them didn't have the best examples in their own lives, but that cannot be an excuse to fail the next generations. God can help us overcome any past deficiencies and move forward.

As we work and walk with the next generation, let us not do all the talking and expect them to listen, or we'll never discover what they're thinking, how they're feeling, and their perception of the situation. We must give them an opportunity to speak. We might even learn something from them in the process. Discern their heart, overlooking any generational perspectives that seem difficult to understand. Let God do the changing.

Do whatever you need to do to welcome and receive them. Show them that you love them and that you are ready to help them achieve their destiny. Jesus is calling for unity and acceptance in the Body of Christ today.

Being a family with many different generations (all with different perspectives on life) is just the normal thing. When you are all from one or two generations, that is what is abnormal. God doesn't want the family divided. He welcomes every generation. If all of you are the same age, and you all see things the same way, what will happen to your church or ministry in the future? Who will lead the family onward when you leave the scene, as we all eventually do?

Bridging the Gap

In this critical season, we must build bridges. It's a time not only to build bridges, but also to bring down the barriers that separate us. Not only do we need to know when to build a bridge; we need the wisdom to know when to burn a bridge. God is doing a brand-new thing. This transitional season is a season of RESET.

I need to build a bridge into the new, and, after I've crossed over, I need to burn the bridge behind me so that when I'm confronted with the emotional challenges of change, I don't go back into the old, the comfortable, the familiar, that I don't take the line of least resistance, but embrace and even fall in love with the challenging new moment in the heart of God that will ensure my destiny and bridge me into legacy.

Each one of us has received a beautiful sound that reaches up to Heaven. We don't all have the same sound, but when we blend all our sounds together in unified worship, suddenly we have an army of God. When we learn to actually prefer one another and care for the welfare of each other and are willing to listen to each other and work together, the result can be wonderful indeed. This is *The Art of Legacy.*

NOT ONLY DO WE NEED TO KNOW WHEN TO BUILD A BRIDGE; WE NEED THE WISDOM TO KNOW WHEN TO BURN A BRIDGE!

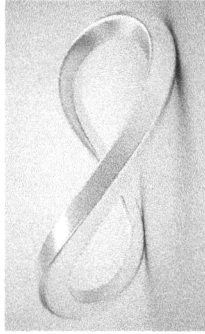

Chapter 5

Reaching the Generations

And this day shall be unto you for a memorial; and ye shall keep it a feast to the LORD throughout your generations; ye shall keep it a feast by an ordinance for ever. Exodus 12:14

Generations interpret things differently, and we must make an effort to understand the new generations and how we can develop with them a healthier relationship and foster better communication. Evangelism is clearly not enough. We need discipleship and plenty of it when it comes to the emerging generations. God is turning the Church upside down so that it will be right side up, and we have to do our part.

What can motivate younger generations to come to church more? What can we do to make them feel more at home when they do come? How can we make them understand that they are an essential part of the Body of Christ, that they have a key role to play in God's plans for the future? These are all things we need to be asking ourselves.

One of the things we may disagree upon generationally is worship. I'm a worshiper. I love to worship, and I feel that our generation has come to understand that we must cultivate worship as a lifestyle. We are also, in general, a bit more demonstrative than younger generations. Some communities are more demonstrative than others. For instance, the Latino communities. Others of us are more "vanilla" in our worship. The important thing is for all generations to learn to worship God in Spirit and in truth. This is a command to all men, not just one or two generations or particular cultures, traditions or backgrounds.

Some have the idea that they don't need to move around in worship, be part of a worship team or even take an active part in worship at all. But the more you can press in during worship, the more you give your heart over to God, the more you demonstrate your love to Him, the more you will receive back from Him. It is just as with any relationship. If I just think in my head how much I love my wife and never tell her, that's not doing much to maintain the marriage relationship. She may know that I love her, but she also loves to hear it. And it's the same with God. He loves it when we express through our worship that we love Him.

In one sense, we are in church as an audience of one, there for the Lord, and if we can set aside everyone else and just focus on Him during that time, the results will be amazing. That's when the creative flow starts, and prophetic words start to manifest and come to the forefront. During that time, you may see a vision or hear the Lord say something to you. Entering into worship is indeed a key to unlocking the greater glory and presence of God.

The higher the praise and the deeper the worship, the greater the glory. Sometimes we don't have enough praise to get over the negative events of the day or to get into the next phase of what we are destined to step into. There must be a shift from praise to worship and then from worship to glory. If we are true to ourselves and God in worship, it will help the newer generations to see that it's okay to be more free in worship.

As a worshiper, I do love to dance, but then, the next moment I may be down on my knees or with my face to the floor. It is fairly unusual these days to see a pastor in his own house on his face before the altar or dancing around. Even though we are all together, I feel like I'm just there before my God. I am worshiping Him, not the people, and I'm not really concerned with everything else that's going on around me because I'm looking for that personal experience.

Each of us has responsibilities in life, and sometimes it is difficult to drop all of that for an hour and really focus on who God is. When we come together to worship, who are we really worshiping? And do we understand why we are worshiping Him? The newer generations must somehow be brought into the realms of worship.

I think we are living in some of the greatest days as far as worship movements have gone. Each generation has lent its own style of music to the mix. It hasn't been all that long ago that worship was done with only an organ. Now we have the drums, the guitars and other instruments, and it is all because of our younger generations and their taste in music.

Reaching the Generations

When I came to the Lord in my mid-twenties, many of the great worship groups, like Hillsong, were not yet active. In the last few decades we have been steadily building a better worship atmosphere in the church, and we owe that to the youth.

These are great times for worship. We have things like Bethel Music, the Jesus Culture, Upper Room Music and other awesome musical elements, and more are to come as we are joined by the next generations.

In one sense, the newer generations don't really know how good they have it. Our worship teams are very professional these days. This has the potential to draw those who are entertainment oriented and to bring them into true worship. The hope is that all generations will become God focused.

The newer generations are very gifted and talented, so one danger for them is to get caught up with individual gifts and fail to really concentrate on worship. Our challenge, as leaders, is to be able to tell the difference between natural talent and the anointing. The anointing, of course, is what will change us all, and these new generations seem to be sensitive to genuineness.

Worship, then, can either be our greatest asset or our worst liability. If we're trying to entertain the young people, we can never rise to the level of worldly entertainment. So, if we're just trying to entertain them, we are bound to be disappointed. If, on the other hand, we can show them something real, they will respond to it.

When there is an anointing in the building where we meet, people feel it the moment they come in the door. As the presence of God begins to fall, they will see there is something different, and it will draw them. If you have experienced it, it's almost like electricity in the air. They may not know what it is at first, but it will raise their curiosity and cause them to investigate further. As we can teach the young that they are entering into the very presence of Almighty God, their lives will be changed.

In modern America, there is so much entertainment, and we in the church feel that we somehow have to compete with that entertainment. There is great music from all genres that we want to do, but we can hardly do it all or do it better than others. Again, the important thing is the anointing. The anointing will cause men and women of all generations to transcend the natural world and move into realms of glory.

There is an anointing on certain songs. Sometimes it may be the song itself, our relationship to it, the anointing upon the musicians who are playing it or those who are singing it. If we can bring the presence of God into our meetings, that will draw everyone into the heavenlies, and lives will be transformed.

The Christian music industry often tends to go with talent rather than anointing, and when this happens, we can immediately tell the difference. We know when something is anointed or when it has been commercialized, and we are not in God's House for entertainment. We are there for the anointing to be birthed in worship.

Many churches do a great job with evangelism, but when it comes to discipleship, nurturing and raising up those who have been birthed into the Kingdom, many fail miserably. These two—evangelism and discipleship—must go hand in hand. No parent would bring a child into the world, only to neglect its need for food, shelter and love afterward. Why do we do that in the church? It's my heart to birth sons and daughters, not orphans.

There is nothing quite like evangelizing, reaching out and touching new people, touching the new generations, touching all those who have not yet experienced the culture of Christ. I love it. But we can't stop there. Far too many people who have been saved are struggling to maintain their walk with Christ simply because they have no one to teach them the ways of God. They love Him and don't want to fail Him, but they have never been properly discipled.

Shockingly, immature people are often placed into leadership positions in churches before they have been discipled themselves. It should surprise no one that they are unable to maintain the needed balance in order to become successful and remain successful spiritually. They never had a chance because someone failed to take them under their wing and show them what the Christian life is all about. What a tragedy!

Billy Graham was one of our greatest evangelists, and many people came to know the Lord through his ministry, but I wonder what percentage of those were properly discipled. Was there someone who took the time and made the effort to teach them what the day-in and day-out life of a believer was like? Did someone show them, by example, what it looks like to walk this thing out? Was someone there to hold them accountable? Was someone there to walk with them and watch to be sure they were doing well spiritually?

Anyone can repeat a sinner's prayer, but not just anyone can know instinctively how to live the successful Christian life. Babies are miraculously born, but for them to grow up and become what they were destined to be takes a lot of effort on the part of dedicated and caring parents. When you and I meet people and witness to them, they often cannot resist our testimony, and so they respond. But who will make sure those same people learn how to walk it out? This is one of the most important failings of my generation.

There is a big difference between the Gospel of salvation and the Gospel of the Kingdom. Many times we preach the Gospel of salvation, and people are moved, but that is just part of the Gospel message. We need to go much deeper, showing men and women how to live in the Kingdom. Being a Christian is a lot more than making an initial decision for Christ or praying a sinner's prayer. It requires your whole life. When we quote Paul, *"I am crucified with Christ: nevertheless I live; yet not I, but Christ liveth in me: and the life which I now live in the flesh I live by the faith of the Son of God, who loved me, and gave himself for me"* (Galatians 2:20), that's just the beginning, the doorway into a whole new life (the Kingdom of God). Who will model this life for the newer generations? Who will love them enough and believe in them enough to teach them step-by-step how to get there?

We have been trained in how to share the Gospel and reach men and women for Christ. Most of us memorized the Roman Road and the Four Spiritual Laws, but can we tell those who come to Christ how to live for Him?

One of the areas where the newer generations are falling down is in the memorization of the Word of God. With us older folks, when we got saved, someone told us how important it was to begin to store up in our hearts God's words, His promises. Just as our modern generations depend on calculators instead of memorizing math tables, they depend on Google when it comes to the Bible, and that is a step backward. There are less students in our Bible schools than there were twenty or thirty years ago, and this is not a healthy trend.

Evangelism is important, and we must not abandon it, but having children and then not caring for those children is irresponsible. Why is it that children grow up so quickly physically, and yet it takes believers many long years to mature into serious Christian adulthood? It's a lack of discipleship and mentoring.

I'm not suggesting that we stop having children. God forbid! I'm suggesting that we get serious with God and start caring for and raising the spiritual children He gives us.

There is a reason God chose to place a variety of ministers and ministries into the Body of Christ. Paul made their role so clear when he wrote:

> *And he gave some, apostles; and some, prophets; and some, evangelists; and some, pastors and teachers; for the perfecting of the saints, for the work of the ministry, for the edifying of the body of Christ: till we all come in the unity of the faith, and of the knowledge of the Son of God, along a perfect man, along the measure of the stature of the fulness of Christ:*

that we henceforth be no more children, tossed to and fro, and carried about with every wind of doctrine, by the sleight of men, and cunning craftiness, whereby they lie in wait to deceive; but speaking the truth in love, may grow up into him in all things, which is the head, even Christ.

Ephesians 4:11-15

We need the prophetic, and we need signs and wonders, but we also need serious teaching. We need all of the fivefold ministries to complete us. And this can't all be done on a Sunday morning. If all we have is Sunday morning worship, we don't have nearly enough. We need teaching and training, and that takes time.

I grew up a Catholic, and all we had was Catechism, but at least I knew the story of Abraham and Sarah, of Isaac and Rebekah and of Jacob and Rachel. I knew about Moses and Joshua and many others of the ancient leaders of faith. It seems that our modern generations are lacking this teaching component, and they need it.

Don't get the wrong impression. Discipleship is not just teaching someone; it is doing whatever is necessary to help them follow Christ.

Reaching the Generations

What did Jesus say in the Great Commission?

*Teaching them to observe all things whatsoever
I have commanded you: and, lo, I am with you
always, even unto the end of the world. Amen.*
                                            Matthew 28:20

We teach in many ways. The most important way we teach is by our example. We also teach as a coach. And then we have the traditional sense of teaching, and that's important too.

What do we teach? *"Teaching them to observe all things whatsoever I have commanded you."* You are responsible to teach everything you have learned. Someone taught you everything, even how to tie your shoes. Will you do the same for the emerging generations?

The younger generations are very experience oriented. They want to feel it and experience it, and I'm all for that. But to be firmly established, every generation must be rooted and grounded in the Word of God. There is no substitute for teaching. The higher I go in revelation, the deeper must be my understanding of the Word. The Word gives us a strong foundation for the power of God and the presence of God. It's all part of keeping ourselves safe. There is power in the Word.

What parent would not teach a child to avoid a hot burner, not to play with matches, to be careful when approaching a high drop off? If we're just being swept along by the river of God, who is to say that our boat is sound? Can we not teach young people to stay in their proper channel? Can we not convince them that when experiencing the prophetic, they must maintain biblical parameters?

Maintaining healthy relationships and observing proper checks and balances within the Body of Christ is so important. Far too many young people read something in the Bible and jump to some wrong conclusion rather than allowing the Spirit to interpret the Word or the Word to interpret itself. We must each have good people around us who can counsel us and speak into our lives.

It is far too easy to take one Bible verse or a portion of one verse out of context and make it mean what we want it to mean or even establish a doctrine all on one verse. We not only need the guidance of the Holy Spirit and the balance of knowing other parts of the Word, but also the help of trusted counselors and teachers. You simply cannot have too many of them.

A mentor might suggest something as simple as, "Did you read the rest of that verse? Did you read the rest of that chapter? Did you read that whole book?" We sometimes have just a small part of the picture, and others can help us gain a fuller view. "Can we look at the scripture before and after to put it all into context?"

All of this, of course, requires a healthy relationship, and we live in such a dysfunctional society with so much brokenness. That's why inner healing is so necessary today. Deliverance is so necessary. Many of our younger generations even need professional and practical counseling. If we don't first deal with their brokenness, their hurts, their habits and their hang-ups, they won't even get to the starting line. Any and all of these things will keep them from being able to move forward in God. If we fail to recognize this in the church and to have an answer for it, we will create, at best, shallow disciples, men and women who are hiding all sorts of sin and brokenness in their personal lives.

Our churches must have a broader and more balanced approach. We must believe in deliverance, we must believe in inner healing, and we must believe in the power of God to set men and women free. But we must also know that there is a component of talking through things and processing things, and we must not shun doctors and other health professionals. We must develop a healthy church by developing healthy relationships across the generations. This requires that we be willing to look at things from various perspectives, always coming back to the foundational truths that will keep us firm.

Every generation is relevant, every generation is important, every generation counts, every generation is worthy of respect, and every generation has something to offer to the rest of us in our journey, our quest, to fulfill the vision and destiny call that is upon our life. Every one of us is essential.

Essential workers is *a* phrase we have been hearing in this time of crisis. To God, and to the Body of Christ, each of us is essential. Each of us is unique. Each of us has something to bring to the table, in communion with Him and with one another. To raise up a generation, we are all essential. This is *The Art of Legacy*.

TO RAISE UP A GENERATION, WE ARE ALL ESSENTIAL!

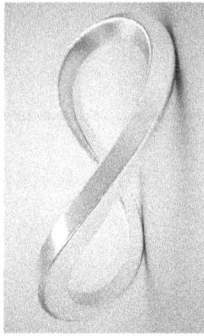

Chapter 6

Divine Appointments, Divine Design

Very truly I tell you, when you were younger you dressed yourself and went where you wanted; but when you are old you will stretch out your hands, and someone else will dress you and lead you where you do not want to go.

John 21:18,NIV

What an honor it is to walk in your destiny, your legacy, your calling and gifting, working with the Lord and His perfect will for your life! What an honor! What an honor it is to serve Him, to walk together and work together with others to achieve a common goal!

I have had many different and wonderful experiences in the various seasons of my life. What a privilege it has been to walk in the presence and anointing and call of God since I was in my mid-twenties! I have been able to experience life in a lot of different spheres of influence. As an athlete, I played ball until I was in my late twenties. I then coached high school football for seven years, and then God put me into business through dreams and visions. He saved me, He delivered me, He set me free, and He brought me into a very unusual place in my life. Every day He has walked with me and worked with me, just as He had promised in Mark 16:19-20:

> *So then after the Lord had spoken unto them, he was received up into heaven, and sat on the right hand of God. And they went forth, and preached every where, the Lord working with them, and confirming the word with signs following. Amen.*

In a moment's time, my life was turned upside down and inside out, and God began to speak to me in dreams and visions. He told me that He would put me into business, and I had never been in business before. I not only had no capital; I also had no business experience or business education. All I had was the Word of the Lord, His personal promise. Sure enough, God established me, and over the years I had several successful businesses until He called me into full-time ministry.

I want you to know that God has a plan and a purpose for your life too. He said:

> *For I know the thoughts that I think toward you, saith the Lord, thoughts of peace, and not of evil, to give you an expected end.*
>
> Jeremiah 29:11

When God speaks something, it is alive, and if you will let it, it will come alive in you. If you will obey God, He will bring you into a place in the visionary realm where you will see things the way He wants them to be. Then He will use you, opening doors for you to pioneer, plow up virgin soil and plant seed. And the fun part is when you begin to reap the resulting harvest.

You don't always see the harvest, but sometimes you have the honor of being there and watching God send the harvesters to reap a harvest from the seed you sowed. Personally, God has sent me many wonderful sons and daughters. Not so long ago, I celebrated my seventieth birthday and had the honor of having a lot of my sons and daughters there for a surprise party. And I was truly and pleasantly surprised.

Like every other prophetic voice, like every man and woman, I struggle, I have insecurities and uncertainties. We're all the same. It has nothing to do with color, culture, foods that you like, things that you do. I've been in just about every kind of situation and people group, and you know what? We may look different, act different and talk different, but when you take us all apart and look inside, you can see the gift of God and the call of God. For each one of us, the individuality that God puts in there is so beautiful. And yet we are all alike in that we all have our weaknesses or shortcomings and need God and His servants to help us mature so that we can fulfill our dreams.

God dynamically allows our paths to cross by divine design. He has brought many people into my life, to walk with me, to work with me, to serve with me and to partner with me in the harvest. He has brought me many sons and daughters, and I have had the honor of seeing God take the seed I sowed into their lives, as

I poured my heart into them, and, with it, He created something beautiful. To see what God has done in the lives of these men and women and see the gift of God and the call of God come alive in them is such a joy.

God sometimes gives me prophetic words for my sons and daughters, and as I speak them, I see them coming alive in their hearts. Next, *they* speak the vision, and then I see the vision becoming reality. What could be more wonderful?

Most of the things that have happened to me in life, especially the big things, came as a result of dreams and visions and revelations, with prophetic confirmations. God speaks to us in dreams, visions, revelations and prophetic confirmations, and I have been blessed to see many of my own dreams come true. Most men and women dream dreams, but a visionary wakes up and sees that dream become a reality. And that's what I always want to do.

There comes a moment when we have to wake up, come down off of the ceiling, stop bouncing off of the walls and running around the mountain and put our feet on the ground, put our hand to the plow and do something to see that dream come to a place of reality. People who do that are not just dreamers; they are visionaries, and they often walk in the visionary realm. Sometimes they walk in an apostolic or prophetic calling as well. Sometimes they walk in a spiritual anointing of God for the church, the government or business.

As I noted, I was successful for many years in sports and then for twenty-one years in business. I was in the security business and ended up with five different companies. I started in the basement of my house with a few hundred dollars and a few friends, and the next thing you know, suddenly I had five businesses and more than two hundred employees. It seemed like it all happened in a moment of time, and I'm sure that other people, when they looked at me, thought, "Wow! What just happened?" But, of course, it doesn't just happen. It happens if you can first see it in your spirit and then walk it out, step by step.

There is so much that goes on behind the scenes, underground (in your heart) that no one ever sees. In building, the foundation takes much time, energy and effort. Nobody sees all that hard work going on, but, then, suddenly, like a candle in the window, the world can see it.

There were a lot of dreams and visions, but there was also a lot of walking together, working together, cooperating with God, with His plan, His purpose, the prophetic word and the revelation that He sent. When you bring it all into alignment in your life and just, somehow or another, put your hand in the hand of the One who can take you into deeper water, it works. I like what Jesus said to Peter:

> *I tell you the truth, when you were young, you were able to do as you liked; you dressed yourself and went wherever you wanted to go. But when you are old, you will stretch out your hands, and others will dress you and take you where you don't want to go.*   John 21:18, NLT

When I was a just a child in the suburbs of Philadelphia, I walked down the street with an attitude. By the time I was twenty, I wondered why the ground didn't shake when I came by. Then I came to the knowledge of Christ, and suddenly my world was turned upside down. My heart was turned inside out, and so was my life. That was fifty years ago, and I'm much older now. When Jesus said to Peter: *"but when you are old you will stretch out your hands, and someone else will dress you and lead you where you do not want to go,"* I believe He was speaking of the Holy Spirit's work in us. I want to always be a man led by the Spirit, given over to the Spirit, madly in love with the Spirit of the living God, the Spirit of Light, the Hope of Glory that dwells within each one of us. I want to hear His voice. I want to know His heart. I want to do His will, His perfect will for me, in every season of my life.

I always want to be in season, and I always want to be on time. I don't want to be delayed by taking detours, especially at this important stage of my life. I want to go right to the mark. I don't want to go around and around the mountain anymore. I want to go up and over the hill and possess the land.

I rejoice in the victories of the Lord, not just in my own life, but also in the lives of my spiritual sons and daughters. I'm a happy man. I may not be as wealthy (from a financial aspect—speaking of dollars and cents) as I was when I was in business, but we very often look at success through the wrong lens. If we look at success from a worldly perspective, then it comes from dollars and cents, praise and recognition. I, for one, am looking for spiritual success.

My goal is the fulfillment of my destiny — why God touched me in the first place, why He called me, what He called me to do, what He is calling me to do in this hour. I want to be in His perfect will. There is a vortex that just seems to sweep you up and suck you in, and you just hope you get there. In God, in the presence of God, in the glory of God, in the purpose of God, there is a place of peace and rest, and you know you are on the right track for success.

There is a reason for every season of our lives, and there is a reason for every individual who comes into our lives. If we expect to be honored, we must honor others. If we expect to reap honor, then we have to sow honor. If I am looking for honor's reward, I have to be a man of honor myself.

Honor is one aspect of our character and our integrity and of our relationships with others. It means that you see the gift and call of God in other people and are honoring them for who they are in Him, not for what they do or what their status in life might be.

It doesn't matter to me if a person is the mayor

of a city, the governor of a state or a humble sanitation worker. They are important and valuable to God and essential to the Body of Christ. They were created in the image of God, to walk in His ways. I must see God in them, and I must honor them for who they are in Him.

I honor the men or women who have poured into my life, those who pioneered before me. I am part of their legacy. I honor those who labor and serve with me now and those into whom I am currently pouring. These younger ones, sons and daughters, will take up their destiny calls and, using the seeds I have sown into their lives, become my legacy. Legacy is about living on after you're gone. Yes, this is *The Art of Legacy.*

Now, receive a fresh anointing, a fresh impartation, a fresh empowerment. Let that apostolic birthing and building anointing come on you, that you may pioneer the new thing that God is doing in this hour and season.

In Jesus' name,
Amen!

I WANT TO HEAR HIS VOICE!

I WANT TO KNOW HIS HEART!

I WANT TO DO HIS WILL!

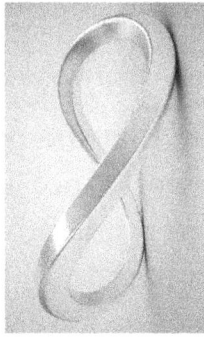

Chapter 7

Your Greatest Harvest Is in Your Seed

While the earth remaineth, seedtime and harvest, and cold and heat, and summer and winter, and day and night shall not cease.

Genesis 8:22

A real visionary knows that the harvest is in the seed. So, when I look at our younger generations, I look at the seed that God has put in them, and I prophesy to that seed. God put it there, and it has great potential. That seed may not look like much right now, but the harvest is in there. Sometimes we connect to the fruit instead of to the root, and we never go back to the seed. Therefore, we don't see the harvest because we've never sowed a seed. If you never sow a seed, you cannot possibly reap the harvest of it.

We must realize that the principle of seed time and harvest works, not just in the area of finances, but in every place of harvest and in every part of your life.

> *And God blessed Noah and his sons, and said unto them, Be fruitful, and multiply, and replenish the earth.* Genesis 9:1

This whole concept is about the power of the seed and the harvest in the seed and about the covenant relationship and perpetual blessing. This is a godly principle that cannot fail. Therefore, as a visionary, I must understand that I need to focus and prepare for the harvest by faith. The moment I sow my seed, I can count on the harvest of it. That seed is an incorruptible one. When it is sown into the Kingdom, it *will* bring forth a harvest.

I need to spiritually see that potential harvest in someone else before my natural eyes actually see it. To do that, I must look past the physical, the outward appearance, and know who they are and what they will do in God. I must do that in every relationship and in every experience.

Because I was birthed in the fires and flames of the Spirit in the midst of revival, I have always wanted to see the power and the presence of God at work. In the early stages of my ministry, I was having some great meetings. Thirteen or fourteen times, my meetings were extended because there was a move of God, and so they went on longer, sometimes for three months, six months, eight months, a year and even a year and a half in one case. I continued to minister every day, three or four times a week or every week in a particular place.

As you can imagine, I was very excited about what I was seeing. Signs and wonders and miracles were present. The gifts and the power of the Holy Spirit were on display. One night, after I had arrived home, I said, "God, thank You so much! What a wonderful meeting!" And, wow, it *was* a tremendous meeting!

Then I heard the Lord say to me, "It's not about meetings."

I said, "Well, thank You for this revival that is happening in the hearts of the people."

He said, "It's not about good meetings. It's not about revival!"

Right about then, I was thinking, "What? It's not about revival?"

Then the Lord spoke to me very clearly, "It's about making sons and daughters!"

I thought God was saying that I would have sons and daughters in this moment of time without much effort on my part. Of course, I was wrong on every count. It takes time and sustained effort to raise up sons and daughters. In this way, the Lord changed my entire perspective on life and ministry and brought me to a generational mindset that matches His cause. He is a generational God.

Soon I began to see that God's purpose was to be fulfilled through discipleship and mentoring and raising up sons and daughters, working from generation to generation to achieve the fullness of the harvest.

This perspective was from the Lord of the Harvest. Now I was seeing the harvest through His eyes. It was a prophetic view, a Kingdom view, and that is the view you and I must see today. He is showing us what is really important.

I began gathering leaders together. I didn't always choose the right ones, even though I prayed very hard about it. It was, at first, an up-and-down thing. I was sometimes taking the time and making the effort to pour into vessels that were not holding the blessing. Some were not able to maintain their stability. They were like a flash in the pan. What was I to do? Then God spoke to me through the Scriptures His plan and purpose:

> *Gather My saints together to Me,*
> *Those who have made a covenant with Me by*
> *sacrifice.* Psalm 50:5, NKJV

Because of this, I began to examine more closely the hearts of the people who were coming my way, and I prayed for the discerning of spirits to help me to see them through God's eyes. Had they really made covenant with God by their sacrifice? Was their desire, their motive genuine? Would they last? Could they stand when the battle got hot? I began to choose the leaders I would pour into in this way, and with this renewed assurance, I began to pour into them with purpose and with zeal. And it worked.

The Lord showed me that I could not lead those who were not willing to follow, that I could not make choices for others. They would not be moved by my desire or my relationship to walk out *their* destiny. They had their own free will and were able to make their own choices. Somehow I had to find those who had made covenant, not just with me, but also with God Himself.

I had to start looking at this journey of life as an opportunity for legacy. The journey was full of twists and turns, detours, hills and valleys. There were even a few off-road experiences, but what a pleasure it would be, reaching for my destiny, my resting place. Suddenly, I knew that this was my calling. This was my destiny.

I would encounter along the way those who were open to my help, and I could form a relationship with them and then lead them onward step by step. These faithful sons and daughters, would be my legacy.

When Daniel Soto, a Costa Rican minister we have been walking with for quite some time now, visited us at our campmeeting in 2019, he said a very beautiful thing: The difference between inheritance and legacy is that an inheritance from your father can be spent in a moment's time, but a true spiritual legacy is for eternity.

There is a great difference between slaves or servants and sons and daughters. Sons and daughters don't work for hire; they work for their inheritance. They are not concerned about their rate of pay or their benefits package. They are coming to answer a call, they're coming with a purpose, and they're coming to claim their inheritance. They realize that they are a child of God themselves and that they are working for their inheritance, so they're willing to invest their heart and soul into everything they do. This is *The Art of Legacy.*

AN INHERITANCE FROM YOUR FATHER CAN BE SPENT IN A MOMENT'S TIME, BUT A TRUE SPIRITUAL LEGACY IS FOR ETERNITY!

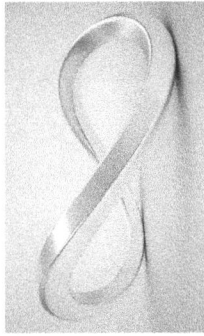

Chapter 8

Fatherhood and Sonship

Behold, I will send you Elijah the prophet before the coming of the great and dreadful day of the LORD: and he shall turn the heart of the fathers to the children, and the heart of the children to their fathers, lest I come and smite the earth with a curse.　　　　Malachi 4:5-6

What an exciting moment we are living in! Things are happening in an accelerated way, at a very rapid pace. We are in the season that every prophet prophesied about. Even Malachi predicted it. God is doing it, turning the hearts of the fathers to the children and the hearts of the children to their fathers. This is an end-time prophecy, and it has to do with fatherhood and sonship and turning hearts back toward each other.

These are the days of Elijah. These are the days of the harvest. The fields are white and ready for harvest.

Jesus is the Lord of the harvest, and you and I were born for the harvest. His heart is for your harvest, and His eye is on your seed. For many of us, our greatest harvest is in our seed. I'm not talking here about seed that can be sown naturally. Every seed you've ever sown—financially, spiritually, emotionally and in every other way—will bear fruit. Once you get the revelation of seedtime and harvest, you will turn everything into seed.

Let's talk about another type of seed—spiritual sons and daughters. I have been blessed to walk with and work with and to raise up and launch out many into their own ministry, gifting and calling. These are ministry seeds that I have sown that will bring forth a great harvest. My heart is that my sons and daughters prosper and do greater works than I ever dreamed of doing. The true heart of a father is this: he wants to be the man his father never was so that his children can be the man or woman he never shall be. He wants them to accomplish more and reap more and to do it with less. He wants them to learn from his mistakes and to build on the foundation that he laid, not having to start over again, but rather to start where he finished. A true father doesn't feel the need to win or to compete with his spiritual children. He wants to stand in faith so that his children can start to build their own lives by standing on his shoulders. They can start where he finished and build a greater house on the foundation that he laid.

What a wonderful season to be alive! It is a prophetic time. Paul wrote to the Corinthian believers:

> *For though ye have ten thousand instructers in Christ, yet have ye not many fathers: for in Christ Jesus I have begotten you through the gospel.* 1 Corinthians 4:15

Recent generations have suffered because of a lack of spiritual fathers and mothers. I suffered that same lack, and it left a void. I was touched by the Lord way back in 1976, but I didn't understand the prophetic or even what a prophet was. When I finally met a few prophets, as I mentioned in an earlier chapter, they seemed to be very mystical, and they would blow in and out of the church. They would minister and then be gone. I thought to myself, *My goodness, they are so spiritual, so incredible,* and what they did felt so wonderful, but it left me empty and void of true relationship and understanding. Somehow I sensed that I had a gift that was not being utilized and that I didn't understand.

I didn't seem to fit into any typical ministerial position because of my prophetic gifting and calling, but I had no one to show me what to do, no one to teach me. The result was that I had to start at the bottom, and thank God for the Holy Spirit and the work He began in my life. Also I thank God for all the men and women He began to send my way—Ruth Heflin; my pastor, Paul Wetzel; Joan Gieson and others—who were able to see and understand something about my gift. They also opened the door for me to receive from others. Then there was Gale and Shelley Sheehan and Bishop Bill Hamon and other great teachers I received from over the years.

As I walked with, talked with and saw in action the fivefold prophetic ministry to the nations and the office of the Prophet operating through the heart and life of Ruth Heflin, these were amazingly powerful personal experiences for me. I grew quickly and was then able to begin teaching prophetic ministry myself.

Over the years, I have raised up hundreds of new prophetic voices. For eighteen years now, we've been doing a School of the Prophets and have traveled around doing a program we have called "The Days of Elijah," equipping and empowering others through seasons of teaching and imparting to them a prophetic anointing. We did this in more than a hundred and fifty churches across North America and around the world. We have also been doing prophetic conferences with teaching, demonstration and impartation that launches prophetic voices into their destiny.

It has been a wonderful journey, a journey of being poured into and then, in turn, pouring into others. It is important that we begin to walk with and work with people who have practical experience in the prophetic so that we can learn to walk in it ourselves.

Of the books I have written to date, my wife Mave thinks that *Living on the Prophetic Edge* is one of the best. It is about understanding the gifts of God, the revelatory gifts in you, and learning how to walk those gifts out in your everyday life, your ministry and your business life.

I also wrote *Leading on the Prophetic Edge,* with teachings on leadership, walking out that leadership anointing and having sound leadership principles, but also sound biblical principles and sound protocol. I have had to walk it out and work it out together with my spiritual family, and it's a wonderful thing to be able to pass all of that on to others.

God is the Giver of the gift, and it's His gift that's imparted to us and through us. In some cases, people began to receive dreams and visions. They began to understand interpretation and application, how to apply their revelations to their lives, how to live by the Spirit and how to be led by the Spirit.

If you are called as a leader in this generation, you need to know how to lead by the Spirit and also how to be led by the Spirit because we are in a time in which we must learn to lead at the speed of change and in the midst of chaos. In this season of crisis, the Pandemic of 2020, and as we go into the "new norm," we must know how to hear the voice of the Lord and be able to teach others to hear Him. More than anything, we must understand obedience and understand fatherhood and sonship. Although I have taught a lot about this in the past, I still have a lot more to learn and a few things to say on the subject.

There is a proper alignment that can prepare a person to receive from others. There was a season in my own life when a spirit of rebellion and pride was on me, and I thought I knew more than others. That is the definition of pride, thinking more highly of ourselves than we ought (see Romans 12:3). Sometimes, because of my life experiences, my business experience or my business sense, if I was dealing with people God had sent into my life who had not had that kind of personal leadership or business success, I found it hard to receive from them. I thought I knew more than they did. The problem was not them. The problem was pride and rebellion in me.

When it comes to learning, the burden of teaching is on the teacher, but the burden of learning is on the student. When the student is ready, the teacher shall appear and will be able to pour into them. When you're green, you're growing. When you're ripe, you're rotten. When you think you know everything, you don't really know anything.

At different times and seasons in my own life, I just couldn't receive from others because I didn't have a spirit of sonship. I just wasn't in the proper position—mentally, emotionally and spiritually—to learn. I didn't have an attitude of humility and an attitude of respect and reverence for the people who were pouring into my life. Respect, discipline and humility are all part of being prepared and properly positioned to receive.

This is all part of preparing good soil in my heart by letting my heart be plowed up and harrowed, so that it was ready to receive seed. That's how you turn yourself into good ground, and I just wasn't good ground at the time. It was not because I wasn't fertile, but because the soil was improperly plowed, and I wasn't rightly aligned.

When I began to see myself going around and around in circles, around and around the mountain, when I had a desire to go up and over the mountain and to achieve and to reach my destiny, then I realized that I needed a spirit of sonship. When I went to God and asked for that spirit with the right heart, I put myself in right alignment and in right attitude, in the right posture of heart and mind, and I was able to receive from those whom God was sending into my life.

These were spiritual fathers, mothers and teachers God wanted to use to bring me to another dimension, another level, another place in the prophetic and in the Spirit. He used them to set me on the launching pad and to launch me forth.

Because of that experience, I have mentored, prepared, equipped and launched countless numbers of other men and women of younger generations and even some older ones. Along the way, there were some who were extremely talented, gifted and capable who simply could not bring themselves into the right posture so that they could be positioned to receive.

Some even called me and said, "You know, Dr. Russ, I really think you are supposed to mentor me." I made an appointment to see them, but when we met, they began to tell me everything they knew, where they had been, and what I should be doing. They clearly were not in a position to receive from me.

I'm afraid that many Christians do that same thing to God. We go to prayer and then insist on telling Him how to bless someone, what to do, what we need, and what we want. Instead of going to Him with a humble heart and a contrite spirit (that He has promised never to despise), instead of humbling ourselves before Him, putting ourselves in a position and posture to listen and receive from Him, we do all the talking and He doesn't have a chance.

I want to pour into hungry vessels. That's my heart, my destiny, my calling, my future. That's my legacy. And I am dedicated to building that legacy. That is my heart's desire, so I am constantly looking for good ground, for people with the right attitude. The wonderful thing is that I learn as much from those whom God sends to me as they learn from me, but that can only happen if my heart is right.

Over the years, my sons and daughters have brought great joy into my life, not just by what they say, but by how they have lived. This would include people like Reid Grassick. I've learned so much from Reid over the years, technical things and things about building, but more importantly, about the gift of servanthood. Just seeing the life Reid lives, how he serves, how he stands, how he walks and what this means to others, I can see the heart of Christ, the heart of the great Suffering Servant in him. I have been able to receive from him.

It would include people like Miguel Simon, another of my spiritual sons. I look at Miguel's life and I see his determination, his willingness to go on and his faith. I have seen him walk through trials and tribulations, hard life experiences and difficult obstacles that life has thrown in his pathway and have observed how he walked, how he lived, how he persevered, how he fought, how he loved. Through him, I've learned to understand enduring faith. I have also learned things about ministry and life.

When I first stepped into missionary ministry in Canada, I had already been doing a lot of deliverance ministry and was taking people through deliverance. Still, I didn't have much of an understanding of inner healing and wasn't looking at it from the right perspective. I had heard of some of the problems that sometimes arose in this type of ministry. Therefore, I was leery of it. Then the Lord sent a wonderful spiritual daughter my way—Patty Thorpe Wallace.

Patty lived with us, walked with us and worked with us in Canada. She began to minister inner healing to some of the people who were receiving deliverance ministry, and I saw the effectiveness of what she was doing. I saw the fruit of it. Those who had gotten free were able to walk in that freedom. Seeing her minister in this way taught me so much.

I have learned from each of these spiritual sons and daughters God has sent into my life, and I have tried to keep my heart in a posture to learn all that I can. That proper posture includes respect, trust, relationship, an openness and willingness to learn and grow, a desire to change, to embrace change and to fall in love with change.

I have come to realize that everyone God sends my way has gifts, talents and abilities. I can learn something from them. Therefore, I must respect the gifting and call of God that's on their life. I must be in the right posture and in the right place at the right time.

I must also learn from those whom God has set in authority over me. I do not let just anybody and everybody speak into my life, but there are people who do speak into my life on a regular basis. Those I believe are God-ordained, I want them to be there, and I want to be accountable to them in every sense of the word. I also want to walk together with my peers. The people of God are designed to walk arm in arm, hand in hand.

Over the years, I have learned from ministers and pastors I've worked with and walked with, but I also want to learn and grow from those God has sent for me to mentor. These are spiritual sons and daughters He put in my life by and for relationship.

I can't tell you how much I've learned from Mave. The love walk she has is absolutely amazing. Because she walks with people and works with people through love, she can then confront issues, circumstances and situations that bring forth change and correction. In the process, she is offering love, hope and expectation. She also taught me a tremendous amount about faith, walking out my faith and living by faith. I believe we can all learn from everyone around us.

Even Jesus, when He went to His hometown and was around His family and friends, found that they were not able to receive from Him. The result was that He could do only a few simple miracles there, nothing like what happened in His ministry throughout other parts of Galilee.

For those who were close to Him, familiarity bred contempt, and it blocked their faith and their ability to receive. They could only look to Him as another person from Nazareth. And, as was said in that day, *"Can anything good come out of Nazareth?"* (John 1:46, NKJV).

Amazingly, the people of Jesus' hometown were blinded by familiarity to the gift of God and the call of God that was on His life, so they were unable to receive from Him.

This same thing happened with Moses and his family. They knew his weaknesses and short-comings. They focused on those, as opposed to the gift of God and the anointing of God that was on his life.

Let us position ourselves emotionally, spiritually, physically, naturally—in every sense of the word. Let us position our hearts to receive everything that God has for us from everyone He sends our way. This is *The Art of Legacy*.

I want to pray for you right now:

May your heart be fertile ground. May you allow the Lord to plow that ground. And may you come with humility to His

table. May you reverence the gift of God and call of God on other people that He sends your way, and may you properly position yourself to receive from them.

Father, I thank You. I thank You for wisdom, discernment and understanding. I pray, Lord, for humility to come to us and respect for those You send to us, so that we would be able to receive every wonderful thing and every blessing they carry. Help us to walk together, to grow together and to flow together from the different streams through the different seasons and times of our lives. We give You all the glory, all the honor and all the praise.

If you are a father, I release upon you an anointing for fatherhood, for patience and strength to parent, to understand and to love.

If you are a mother in the Spirit, I speak into you that mighty anointing and spirit of motherhood that can speak life, hope, strength, encouragement and correction into others.

If you are a son or daughter, my prayer for you, my declaration today is that a spirit of sonship or daughterhood would rest upon you, that you would be positioned properly to receive from everyone in your life, that you would be receptive, that you would be good ground, that your heart would be properly prepared so that the seed could bring forth its fruit and that you would be planted by the river and bear fruit in every season.

In Jesus' name,
Amen!

THE BURDEN OF TEACHING IS ON THE TEACHER, BUT THE BURDEN OF LEARNING IS ON THE STUDENT. WHEN THE STUDENT IS READY, A TEACHER SHALL APPEAR!

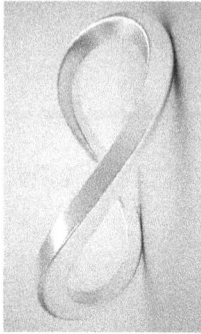

Chapter 9

Don't Throw Caution to the Wind
(WORDS OF WISDOM)

Above all else, guard your heart,
for everything you do flows from it.

Proverbs 4:23, NIV

In this chapter, I want to share some wisdom principles for mentoring and parenting, as well as some building strategies that will bring understanding to the process.

Proverbs 4:7 says:

Wisdom is the principal thing;
Therefore get wisdom.
And in all your getting, get understanding.

NKJV

Certainly, as a mentor and a builder in the Kingdom of God, we need wisdom and understanding. Yes, wisdom is the principal thing. But verse 23 clearly tells us *"above all else."* This means even above wisdom, guard your heart. We must establish healthy relationships and boundaries because the work of a builder in the Kingdom is a matter of the heart. Everything flows from that place of legitimate relationship.

Many young and emerging leaders have come our way over the years, and some, because of the nature of our ministry, giftings, anointing or the growth they have seen or experienced, have asked us to mentor them. This has been done in many different ways—through teaching and training online, in live seminars, at our camp schools or through an involvement with some of our local churches where we partner with our spiritual sons and daughters to train and equip, empower and launch believers. Of course, they must then continue the process we consider foundational and critical to the New Testament model and the heart of the Lord.

Having the wisdom and foresight to know how, when, where and with whom to engage is essential. It all takes time and the commitment of all the parties involved. It's important that it be a positive experience. Therefore, setting some healthy boundaries and realistic expectations at the outset are important in your quest for success.

A wise leader, father and mentor has to be able to recognize and deal with at least three types of individuals that seriously engage the leader with a desire to be mentored so that they know at what level of relationship they are to connect, in order to avoid unhealthy relationships and disappointments. Time is one of our most valuable commodities in mentoring and parenting, and the object is to invest it wisely, not just spend it.

Apostle John Kelly, the Convening Apostle of the International Coalition of Apostolic Leaders, has been a mentor and spiritual father to me. He is a powerful leader and a man of great wisdom. He saw my heart and knew I was struggling and taught me a lot about legacy, leadership and mentoring. He said, "Apostles are both fathers and generals." His biggest mistakes, he told me, came in situations where he should have reacted like a father and, instead, reacted like a general or when he should have reacted like a general and, instead, reacted like a father.

While I was living at the Calvary Pentecostal Camp in Ashland, Virginia in the summer of 2000, a prophetic leader named Gerard Habestro spoke a very timely and strategic word of wisdom and knowledge into my heart about mentoring sons. I had just left a group of powerful young men I had been mentoring for more than two years in Pensacola, Florida. I was sad and concerned with my progress, but I hadn't told anyone what I was going through. As I came off the platform after a morning service, he said to me, "You are troubled about some young men you have left behind, but the Lord knows that and will care for them. They are His and were birthed in the Spirit. I, the Lord will give you sons and daughters wherever I send you and will give you wisdom and discernment in the future so that you will be pouring into worthy vessels that will contain the blessing."

I have learned that to successfully select those you work so closely with, you must pray and have good discernment, and you must know the difference between a protégé, a prodigal and a parasite! Each of these types will show up in different moments and seasons, and most of them will say all the right things. The key is to know how to recognize them and what to do with them?

THE PROTÉGÉ

A protégé is "a person who is guided and supported by an older and more experienced or influential person." A good biblical example is Elisha, who was an aide and protégé of Elijah and was mentored or trained by him. This relationship bore great fruit and had lasting results. Until the moment of transition occurred, in his waiting moments, Elisha remained faithful to Elijah. Then, when he first received the mantle, in his first assignment he was referred to as "the one who served or poured water on the hands of the prophet." He considered that to be an honor, and it opened the first door for him. Elijah had a whole company of prophets he taught and mentored, but the relationship with Elisha started special and finished well.

THE PRODIGAL

In the biblical parable of the Prodigal Son, the prodigal son received his inheritance and traveled to a distant country, wasting all his money in wild extravagance. Becoming desperately poor, he then returned to his father and was received with open arms.

Prodigal, here and elsewhere, means "rashly or wastefully extravagant." I've had many prodigals that turned out wonderfully and, of course, some who didn't. They all captured my heart, but a few also broke my heart. The process itself is a risky emotional business, but no risk, no gain; no pain, no gain.

THE PARASITE

A parasite is "an organism that lives in or on another organism of another species (its host) and benefits by deriving nutrients at the other's expense." This type of person can be quite dangerous and can cause great harm, even inadvertently. So parasites must be handled with great care. Remember, however: these are also sons or daughters of the Lord, and He loves them. They are, many times, a part of your learning experience and, almost always, a test before promotion. They must be treated well and with respect.

How do I recognize each of these groups and appropriately respond to them?

RECOGNIZING AND DEALING WITH THE PROTÉGÉ

In the case of the protégé, pour out freely of yourself, your knowledge, your wisdom and your experience. He or she will receive it with joy and put it to good, practical and fruitful use for Kingdom purposes and the common good, as well as personal advancement and achievement. The protégé will honor his or her mentor and be proud of the relationship. He or she will return to share the victory and spoils and will cultivate the relationship.

This relationship is mutually beneficial, and each is respectful of the other's time, schedule, personal commitments and vision. You should encourage, affirm and support one another.

RECOGNIZING AND DEALING WITH THE PRODIGAL

With the prodigal, you must trust but be careful when pouring into them. Do it with care and in the proper measure. If you give it all at once, they may take it and waste their inheritance on worldly and perishable things, things which bring joy for a season but have no eternal benefit.

The prodigal is, many times, a "feel-good" oriented person, and they gather their pleasure from their leisure rather than from their work. Their personalities can be exciting and attractive and cause you to lead with your heart and pass right by some important warning signs. Their focus is "me, me, me," and everything is "now, now and now!" Therefore, in short order, they will find themselves empty and shipwrecked.

The prodigal has a tendency to be "all in" at the beginning, but you must let them go when they want to leave. If not, they can cause great harm. Their selfish perspective and powerful personalities can cause more harm than good in the family. Because of their son status, prodigals have influence that can be both positive and negative. You, as the mentor, will find yourself disappointed and discouraged in this process, but when they return and truly repent, we must meet and greet them with open arms, celebrate their return and restore them back into the family with all the benefits of sonship. We must have wisdom as well and realize that, at times, you can have reconciliation but not restoration ... until the prodigal is ready and willing and has learned the important lessons of faithfulness.

RECOGNIZING AND DEALING WITH THE PARASITE

With the parasite, he or she is a one-way street and can, many times, only form unhealthy relationships. They take and take and never get enough. Many times they are barren and dishonoring. They live off of the mentor and often will drain them of needed nourishment that could be used for true sons and daughters. They are self-centered. They seem to repeat the process over and over in one or multiple settings or relationships. Many of them have an orphan spirit, going from place to place. They transfer from host to host, taking full advantage of the opportunities of the moment for quick advancement, using relationships and name dropping to gain influence and access to individuals for the quick success they crave.

Unhealthy and ungodly ambition is a telltale sign and a dead giveaway of parasites. A lack of loyalty and broken covenant relationships are also recognizable signs. However, with them, we must truly discern. Often, we are unable to recognize these signs because we are blinded by our love for the person.

With the parasite, the mentor must know that this relationship is unhealthy and separate from the person or suffer the consequences. You have to rid yourself of a parasite or it will eat all offered nourishment and drain the life out of you.

With these individuals, you must establish healthy boundaries and limits. You must know when enough is enough, thereby protecting the rest of those you are working with, or they, too, can begin to adopt this same pattern as acceptable and can, thus, cause you to taint positive and valuable relationships.

Many times, those who are parasites will, at first, seem like an answer to prayer with great potential—talent, ability and skills. Of course, they sell and present themselves well. They gather people to themselves and bring division to your group. They operate in a spirit of Absalom, with criticism of the leader and flattery of others that causes them to break covenant.

When this spirit of Absalom is at work, it is self-promoting, and the individual feels unappreciated or misunderstood by leaders, as if they have been passed over for promotion, isolated and separated. Like Absalom, they sit near the gate and pick off people at some vulnerable point of change or transition, pointing out how they would not have treated an individual the way the leader did if they were in charge.

Regardless of the risks or dangers involved, we are all called to disciple. That is made clear in the Great Commission of Matthew 28:19. We are all commanded to *"make disciples."* We are to love everyone, but we can choose whom we walk with in covenant relationship.

Even though we are all called to disciple, we are not all called to mentor and father everyone. Each of us has different gifts, talents and abilities. Those of us who are called to mentor must have the wisdom, discernment and grace to walk out the personal parenting process. We must also be willing and obedient to take the time and have the patience this requires. We must know when to build bridges and when to burn bridges, when to hold on and when to let go in relationships!

When we hold on to a relationship beyond its time, it can become toxic. We need wisdom to understand the times and seasons because there is a time and season for everything. Solomon, in all his wisdom and under the influence of the Spirit, said:

Ecclesiastes 3:1-8, NKJV

To everything there is a season,
A time for every purpose under heaven:

A time to be born,
And a time to die;
A time to plant,
And a time to pluck what is planted;
A time to kill,
And a time to heal;
A time to break down,
And a time to build up;
A time to weep,
And a time to laugh;
A time to mourn,
And a time to dance;
A time to cast away stones,

And a time to gather stones;
A time to embrace,
And a time to refrain from embracing;
A time to gain,
And a time to lose;
A time to keep,
And a time to throw away;
A time to tear,
And a time to sew;
A time to keep silence,
And a time to speak;
A time to love,
And a time to hate;
A time of war,
And a time of peace.

We, as natural and spiritual parents, must listen closely to the Master Builder. There is also a time for tough love, but we must pick our battles. If we fight every battle, like betting on every horse in the race, we will have many more losers than winners.

In Proverbs 1:2-7, we are instructed:

To know wisdom and instruction,
To perceive the words of understanding,

Don't Throw Caution to the Wind

To receive the instruction of wisdom,
Justice, judgment, and equity;
To give prudence to the simple,
To the young man knowledge and discretion —
A wise man will hear and increase learning,
And a man of understanding will attain wise
counsel,
To understand a proverb and an enigma,
The words of the wise and their riddles.

*The fear of the L*ORD *is the beginning of knowledge,*
But fools despise wisdom and instruction.

NKJV

The beginning of wisdom is the fear of the Lord. In Proverbs 3:1-7, we are again instructed:

My son, do not forget my law,
But let your heart keep my commands;
For length of days and long life
And peace they will add to you.
Let not mercy and truth forsake you;
Bind them around your neck,
Write them on the tablet of your heart,
And so find favor and high esteem
In the sight of God and man.

Trust in the LORD with all your heart,
And lean not on your own understanding;
In all your ways acknowledge Him,
And He shall direct your paths.

Do not be wise in your own eyes;
Fear the LORD and depart from evil.   NKJV

I hope this helps you, as you begin to recruit, mentor and parent you own team, tribe and family. You cannot always readily and fully recognize these various types until their behavior begins to manifest and indicates the spirit and motive behind the person. You must live justly, love mercy and walk humbly with your God and with those He has entrusted into your care.

In a season when I was disappointed with my selection of leaders and individuals I was mentoring and the results I seemed to be producing for the effort I was putting out, as I noted earlier in the book, the Lord gave me this verse as a selection guide:

Gather My saints together to Me,
Those who have made a covenant with Me by
sacrifice.   Psalm 50:5, NKJV

My prayer for you today is that the Lord would give you revelation, wisdom and understanding! Solomon, when he took the throne, did not ask for the heads of his enemies or for silver and gold, but for wisdom to lead God's people.

Lord, who could lead Your people without wisdom? Lord, grant us wisdom, patience, courage and strength!

WE MUST ESTABLISH HEALTHY RELATIONSHIPS AND BOUNDARIES BECAUSE THE WORK OF A BUILDER IN THE KINGDOM IS A MATTER OF THE HEART!

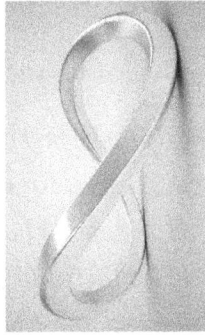

Chapter 10

Learning from Loved Ones

Wives, submit to your own husbands, as to the Lord. For the husband is head of the wife, as also Christ is head of the church; and He is the Savior of the body. Therefore, just as the church is subject to Christ, so let the wives be to their own husbands in everything.

Husbands, love your wives, just as Christ also loved the church and gave Himself for her, that He might sanctify and cleanse her with the washing of water by the word, that He might present her to Himself a glorious church, not having spot or wrinkle or any such thing, but that she should be holy and without blemish. So husbands ought to love their own wives as their own bodies; he who loves his wife loves himself. For no one ever hated his own flesh, but nourishes and cherishes it, just as the Lord does the church. For we are members of His body, of His flesh and of His bones. "For this reason a man shall leave his father and mother and be joined to his wife, and the two shall become one flesh." This is a great mystery, but I speak concerning Christ and the church. Nevertheless let each one of you in particular so love his own wife as himself, and let the wife see that she respects her husband.

Ephesians 5:22-33, NKJV

I have lived a wonderful life. I would even call it a charmed life, and I am a happy and fulfilled man. I've experienced many different seasons in this journey of life, and God has ordained many wonderful people to help me—walking with me and working with me—men and women He sent my way to mentor me and to disciple me, to equip me to lead in different areas of life, including youth, sports, business and entertainment, and, of course, ministry. What a wonderful journey it has been!

Every season of my life has been a blessing, but I am now in the season when I reflect occasionally and also have the freedom to say what's on my heart. As we get a little further along in life, we often know our own minds better. I am excited about this season of life, and I'm doing a lot of talking about legacy, about fatherhood, sonship, paternity, parenthood, all the things that have to do with family.

We have a spiritual family—the Church—and we also have a natural family, and I can say that family is the heart of God and the root of what He is trying to do and say in the earth today. It all has to do with relationship, and it has to do with learning and growing and understanding and maturing. These are all beautiful and wonderful things that we often don't take enough time to talk about or communicate about.

Sometimes we're in such a hurry, chasing our dreams, going after the things of this world, and these consume our heart. But sometimes, while we are pursuing these things, more important things are going on around us, and yet we fail to take time to smell the roses. We can't see the forest for the trees. We don't take the time to ponder on the larger, the greater and the grander things of life.

As I have noted, the events of the last four or five years have radically changed the focus of my thinking. I have been spending much more time considering what is most important in life. I have also started taking time, in the midst of my vision quest, to see what others are going through, and the result is that the quality of my life has improved dramatically. My attitude and perspective are healthier than they've ever been. I can now appreciate the good, the bad and the indifferent. In every condition that I find myself, whether it be one of need or of abundance and plenty, I am blessed in every season and am comfortable with who I am, what I'm about and what I'm currently doing.

Some wonderful things come to us when we reach a place of maturity. We may no longer have the same physical energy and strength, but we have so much more in wisdom and discernment. The quality of our life can improve dramatically, and the quality of the relationships around us can find their right level and their right positioning.

As I said, I learned from all those who poured into my life, mentoring me and discipling me in life—my coaches, parents and leaders and all the teachers who have gone on before me. I have also learned from those whom I have mentored, taught, walked with and worked with. My spiritual sons and daughters have taught me so much, but I also learned from my peers and know that God put them in my life with covenant relationship for a purpose.

Probably the one peer who has taught me more and been the greatest blessing in my life, other than Jesus Himself, is Mave Moyer, my wife. What a wonderful woman of God, wife, mother and friend Mave is! So many different relationships are wrapped up in this one person, and she is just a beautiful person.

Mave is a woman of great wisdom and a woman of the Word. She is also a person of great love and, through her, I have been able to experience that love more and observe it more. I am enthralled by the way she deals with and handles people in her life circumstances and situations. She has been a great pleasure to be with, and what an honor and a privilege it has been for me to share this journey with her, one of the greatest blessings in my life. In this chapter, I want to share with you some of the things Mave has taught me.

Mave has taught me about accountability and relationship and how they relate to spiritual and natural things, particularly focusing on areas of ministry. Mave says that ministry is a sacred trust between God, the leaders of each ministry and those who follow us as we follow Christ. These are precious people who have been entrusted to us by the Lord, and we are responsible to teach them the truth from the Word of God.

Mave is a woman of the Word. She loves to teach how the Word can keep people safe and how it can help them to fully receive the transformational touch of God. This is not a right; it's a privilege.

The apostle Paul showed us by example his accountability to the council in Jerusalem. I'm not sure why so many of us think or feel there is no need for accountability today. The truth is that we need accountability more than ever before.

We are in a very difficult season, a time of war and roses, a season of battle and love and family, and there is a near torrent of good and evil, fighting one another and God. Still, for the believer, God uses proper alignment to protect us every step of the way. He positions us properly in the Body so that we can receive from those

He has placed in our lives and we can mature as sons and daughters, having the right godly alignment and protection of positioning to be prepared and equipped.

Many ministries today suffer from rebellion and detach themselves from any relationship that includes correction or accountability. They make decisions independent of any oversight and many times end up hurting themselves and those who follow them. Accountability and spiritual alignment are wonderful things. They help to shape and to sharpen us and to keep us out of harm's way. As we yield and listen to those God has brought into our lives as a place of wisdom and safety, we are protected.

Mave, in her ponderings that she puts out daily on Facebook and in all her other teachings, has much to say on accountability. Admittedly, accountability presents some troubling issues and some difficult things to walk through, but that's all part of our making and molding, and God has a blessing in it. He is helping to shape us, sharpen us and keep us from error. Therefore, we must yield and listen to those He has brought into our lives as a place of wisdom and safety, accountability and alignment. This is a biblical concept that is much needed in the Body of Christ today, for it produces true sons and daughters.

Sons and daughters are themselves destined for the purpose of paternity and maternity. We must know who we are and what we're about and how we fit or where we belong. This helps us to rightly connect and be in line with the people who can help us to reach our full potential.

God has a plan for *your* life and that plan includes a spiritual family. This is His spiritual means of alignment, the same way He planned our growth in the natural family setting. As Mave noted, Ruth needed Naomi to reach her destiny, Timothy needed Paul, and Elisha needed Elijah. True alignment is not about some better person controlling us; it's about having a more seasoned spiritual parental figure in our lives to provide loving encouragement and wise counsel.

A true parental influence wants us to succeed above and beyond anything they have had. We need the influence of a mentor who can see our need and stir up the gift of God in us, the abilities of God, the talents of God, the potential of God, that we might be established in the ministry we are called to.

Learning from Loved Ones

We have all said, at one time or another, that Jesus is Lord, but is He King and Lord of your life, implying authority and obedience? Too often we don't align ourselves with His Word when it comes to being in right relationship with other people. We all love Jesus as Savior, but what about as Lord? Is He truly the Lord of our lives? That requires something of us. It confronts our independence and tendency to be on our own and causes us to be accountable to the Word of God and to one another, that we might become mature in Christ.

The Word of God is relevant in every culture and every tradition, every tribe, every tongue and every nation. The Word of God works and is relevant in every situation. Everything in the world around us may change, but the standard of the Gospel of Jesus Christ, the Gospel of the Kingdom, will never change. Like Jesus, it is the same yesterday, today and forever. Because the God who put the Word into place changes not, it is time to get into a God-ordained relational alignment for our divine assignment and to bear fruit and fruit that lasts in the Kingdom.

It is important that we yield to the Spirit of God, to the timing of God, to the purpose of

God, to the plan of God. It is time that we become willing to change and to move and to flow with what God is doing in our generation. It's time to honor those who pour into our lives so that we can receive honor and rewards. And it is time to honor and respect those who walk with us and those we have been called to mentor and lead. Love is the answer, and love is based on honor, respect, truth and honesty, foundational truths of solid relationships.

It is important that we take a good hard look at who we are, where we are, what we're doing, and what we're called to do. This is a time for us to seek the Lord with all our hearts and all our soul, to seek Him now like we've never sought Him before, to seek Him in a place of intimacy and relationship. It is also time to begin to develop those other relationships that He has ordained for us, so that He can position us where He can prosper us and propel us into the great harvest that is even now on the way.

Now's the time, the time to embrace change, to fall in love with change, the time to allow God to alter our path and bring us to that great relationship with Him in Word and in Spirit, in praise and worship and honor, to praise Him in the beauty of holiness, to fall in love with change in our own lives. It is time to turn again and follow hard after God, for we are moving into a new season, one of great revelation, a wonderful season of visitation and habitation, a season in which God is raising up torchbearers who will bring a revelation of the knowledge of the glory of the Lord wherever they go, so that the whole earth will be covered with His glory.

We are moving into a season in which the presence of God will be very strong and very tangible. We will experience supernatural restoration, resurrection and the power of Christ among us, doing greater things than ever happened before, even in the book of Acts. The greatest season in the history of the Church is upon us now. This is our greatest moment, the unveiling of the mature sons and daughters of God for whom all of creation has been waiting, and the best is yet to come. This is *The Art of Legacy*.

TO FULFILL MY DESTINY, IT'S NOT ENOUGH JUST TO ENDURE CHANGE OR EVEN EMBRACE CHANGE; I MUST FALL IN LOVE WITH CHANGE!

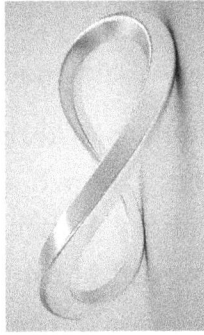

Chapter 11

A Sacred Trust

Because the creature itself also shall be delivered from the bondage of corruption into the glorious liberty of the children of God. For we know that the whole creation groaneth and travaileth in pain together until now. And not only they, but ourselves also, which have the firstfruits of the Spirit, even we ourselves groan within ourselves, waiting for the adoption, to wit, the redemption of our body. Romans 8:21-23

In this chapter I want to further address the all-important issue of spiritual fatherhood and paternity as it relates to the art of legacy and living on after you're gone. Fatherhood, motherhood, parenthood, sonship and daughterhood ... these are very prophetic and timely subjects that can teach us what we need to do to be able to pour into others and what we need to do to receive from others. Spiritual mothers and fathers have an important role to play in God's Kingdom.

Daniel Soto has a wonderful revelation on paternity and fatherhood. The first time he spoke of paternity I didn't quite grasp the depth of the word. I had heard this term only in relationship to a man receiving a paternity test. *Paternity* is a legal term, meaning "the state of being someone's father." Usually, the man is denying that he is the father, and he has to take the test to prove it.

As I have noted, our younger generations are somewhat fatherless, and my generation hasn't done much to help them. Parenting takes time and effort, and so many of our young people have not been properly parented. Some have been parented, but wrongly, and this leaves them with the hurt and pain of control, manipulation and abuse. Others were rejected and abandoned or even orphaned, so they were never really parented at all. Whether you had no parenting or bad parenting, it leaves you struggling to find your right place and correct alignment as a spiritual son or daughter. Having a right relationship with God becomes a chore for some because the only thing that has been modeled to them is a perverted human version of fatherhood, and they are left with their hurts, pains and insecurities.

Uncertainty can cause us to be in a wrong posture to be able to receive. We are afraid to even come into relationship, and even a simple word of correction in love can birth a negative response from our hearts and open up old wounds from the past. But we must persist, for the Kingdom of God is about multiplication.

When Daniel first came to our church and began speaking about paternity, I felt that we already had a good revelation of fatherhood and sonship, having practiced both in life and in ministry. Because of my many years in business and in coaching young people in football, my heart had always been to work with the next generations. And yet when Daniel spoke of paternity, I realized that there was more to the word than I had at first thought.

When Daniel ministered a fresh and healthy revelation of paternity, I realized that this was the heartbeat for our hour. To be a good parent,

I must have the heart of the Father. I must have an understanding of being loved myself, of being accepted and received and being comfortable in my own identity, before I can really fully pour into others.

There is an identity crisis occurring all over the earth today, and part of that identity crisis is that there's a lack of paternity. We don't know whose child we are, and we don't know the responsibilities of being a child and a member of the family. We don't know the responsibilities and duties of a parent because we have never seen anyone model that for us.

We have now crossed the threshold of two or three generations that have not been properly linked together in the right heart and the right attitude. Therefore, instead of producing sons and daughters, we have produced orphans. There is an orphan spirit at work in the church today. People are afraid of being parented because of the hurts and pains of the past. If they cannot somehow get a revelation of sonship, they will never be an integral part of the church.

Some go to church because it's the thing to do, and they know it's important. They know it's the right place to be. They feel good going to a church, and they'll join the church and attend services. They'll even join a group in the church and, in this way, become a part of the church. But, if they don't get the revelation of paternity, of fatherhood and sonship, if they don't get the revelation of who they really are, they will be haunted by that orphan spirit so that they never really know whose they are, how they fit in or if they really do belong. The result is that men and women today are incapable of setting up healthy boundaries and relationships that will bear the fruit of identity.

The reason there is an identity crisis in the world today is because there's an identity crisis in the church, and it's been there now for several generations. Some of us came from parental oversight and were parented with a heavy hand of discipline, without relationship correction, and that produces rebellion, fear, hurt and pain, and also intrudes on healthy and good relationships that God is trying to establish for us in the Body of Christ, which is the family of God. This affects every area of our lives, and the next thing you know, we're not able to multiply in a healthy way.

God is working to bring formation to the Church. His Kingdom is about organization, discipline and structure, as much as anything else. It's a governmental place of truth and formation.

We need to gain an understanding of humility, not a false humility, but a true humility that will help position us properly to prosper spiritually, mentally, emotionally and physically. We must grow, mature and come into our own, having a well-balanced relationship with our peers, with our spiritual leaders, our mentors, and with those we, in turn, are discipling and mentoring.

To have the proper boundaries in place, we need to understand who we are in Christ and who Christ is in us. All of creation is waiting, as Paul wrote:

> *Because the creature itself also shall be delivered from the bondage of corruption into the glorious liberty of the children of God. For we know that the whole creation groaneth and travaileth in pain together until now. And not only they, but ourselves also, which have the firstfruits of the Spirit, even we ourselves groan within ourselves, waiting for the adoption, to wit, the redemption of our body.* Romans 8:21-23

A Sacred Trust

We need mature sons and daughters to rise up who understand who they are in Christ, knowing their identity, what they're called to, how they fit and why they belong. Mature ones no longer question themselves at every step in their quest and are no longer double-minded in their ability to receive and to give. The hurt and broken are unable to walk in obedience because of double-mindedness and insecurity.

Some, because they don't have relationship with the Giver of a gift, lean only on the gift and not the Giver. They don't yet understand fully being loved for who they are and not for what they do. They are sometimes unable to live life from any place other than ambition and greed, a desire for things, fortune and fame. They have been trained to use *something* to fill their empty places. That emptiness comes from not knowing who they are in God, who He is in them and that they are indeed loved and received. This gives the enemy an opportunity to attack them. It is important that we all get a serious understanding of paternity.

In the Christian life, every day is Father's Day, and we must find the heart of the Father and know that His love is different than the man-made variety. God's love is not based on my performance, behavior or achievements. It is unconditional. He loves me for who I am, and I can love Him for who He is in me. Then we can begin to multiply and bear the fruit of healthy offspring.

The Pharisees sought the best places at the feasts, the most important seats in the synagogue or the greetings of the people in the marketplace—all to feed their insecurities. I can be at peace with who I am and how God made me, and I am willing to do more without there being a focus on *me*.

How good it is that God is so faithful. And just to think that He is my Father, and I am not an orphan. You might recognize those orphan spirits in your midst. They can look a lot like a son and can be in the position of a son, but because of their hurt, their pain and their need, they are not able to receive and are incapable of relating in a proper way. This affects their actions and their reactions. It turns them into vagabonds, and they go from place to place and person to person, looking for that someone special.

Far too many are looking for someone in the spotlight, some celebrity personality, to walk with, but that's not the way God does it. He alone chooses who we walk with and work with. People in the spotlight, those celebrity personalities, may not have enough time to parent you and me.

There is nothing wrong with being in the spotlight. We all do what we are called to do, but there are people who are ordained and put in place specifically for the purpose of mentoring me. I just need to have the right attitude, the right position in my heart. I have to make myself available. I have to submit to authority. I have to walk with the right people and talk with the right people. I have to be open. I have to be vulnerable. I have to be trusting. If there is no foundation of truth, honesty, respect and vulnerability in me, I will gain little from such a relationship.

In any relationship, many things have to be cultivated, and if I am not in a healthy spiritual condition, I won't be willing to make the effort to cultivate that relationship. It takes effort. There are many who, no matter what we say or do, will not be willing to accept our spiritual friendship. We just can't get through to them, and it's because they are not ready for it. So, off they go, from one place to another, and in the process, they cause much hurt and pain.

It is painful to have spent the time and made the effort to pastor, mentor and parent those who are not ready to grow up and be serious individuals in the Kingdom. We pour into them for a time, and then off they go, often offended, hurt and broken, and the mentor, the parent, also feels this hurt. This is my child, my son, my daughter, and I am unable to help them.

There are, of course, two sides to every story, and we must view this phenomenon from both sides. In the end, it all comes down to a place of alignment, knowing, first and foremost, that I am a son of Almighty God, and then choosing to walk in alignment in and with the rest of His blessed family.

I need a relationship with God, and I also need a relationship with men and women of God. This will assure that the call placed on my life is fulfilled. This is so important. Have you found your right place in God and among the people He has ordained for your life? Can you walk with Him and with them through the difficult moments of covenant relationship, covering relationship, parental relationship? We must do this without aborting the process.

Aborting the process is part of the enemy's plan. As you're trying to walk out this wonderfully blessed covenant relationship, which will bring forth a commanded blessing of unity, the enemy tries his best to release the spirit of sabotage on the relationship, so that you will abort your position of sonship and, with it, your eternal destiny.

Be careful, for the enemy hates you and will press you on every side. Don't allow yourself to be easily offended. Insist on standing your ground and working your way through any issues that arise. Be open to dialogue and communication. Don't sulk in silence; speak out. This is important to paternity.

Paternity is for eternity, and I want you to know that you are, in fact, a son or daughter of the living God. He loves you, cares for you and cares about you. This is *The Art of Legacy*.

My prayer for you is that you will establish the right and proper relationships and attitude and heart posture that will allow you to stay in your place and mature. Stay in your place, and you will receive just and due rewards. Get your roots down

deep and begin to bear fruit and fruit that lasts. Allow yourself to be discipled and mentored, prepared and equipped for the greatest harvest ever.

I wish you the very best in God. Now, in closing, I release a blessing over you and your family. May the peace of Shalom that grows beyond all understanding cover you as you stand in your new place in Him.

In Jesus' name,
Amen!

GOD'S LOVE FOR ME IS NOT BASED ON PERFORMANCE, BEHAVIOR OR ACHIEVEMENTS. THIS LOVE IS UNCONDITIONAL!

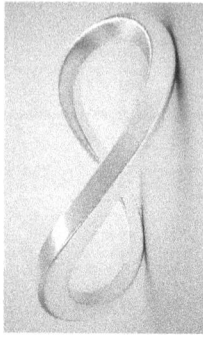

Chapter 12

Effectively Running the Race

Behold, how good and how pleasant it is for brethren to dwell together in unity! It is like the precious ointment upon the head, that ran down upon the beard, even Aaron's beard: that went down to the skirts of his garments; as the dew of Hermon, and as the dew that descended upon the mountains of Zion: for there the LORD commanded the blessing, even life for evermore.

Psalm 133:1-3

All across the nations of the world, God is bringing a great transition, a generational transition. He is a generational God. He is the God of Abraham, He is the God of Isaac, and He is the God of Jacob. That requires fathers to sow into the lives of their children and grandchildren, and it requires children and grandchildren to take hold of the things that are entrusted to them by former generations. God is the God of all generations, and He is finally bringing us together in this season so that we can walk and work and live together, so that we can prosper and grow and be all that He has called us to be.

We are all in different seasons of life, and it just so happens that I am in the season of legacy. Each of us is on a spiritual journey, and you may be at a different stage of your journey than I am. The stark truth, however, is that all of us will one day pass from this scene, and a new generation will take our place. Are we preparing for that eventuality? Are we preparing those who must step into our shoes?

From the moment God first touched you, He has been working out His plan for your life here on this earth. You will move from stage to stage, but inevitably you will find yourself, like me, looking back on life and being concerned about what will happen when you are no longer here. That is the time to be sure you have left an enduring legacy. This season of legacy is nothing to fear; it is the greatest season of life.

Some Christians consider this matter of legacy to be "too secular." It's not. It's a matter of leaving fruit that lasts, leaving fruit that crosses generations and continues even after we are gone from the scene.

I am the fruit of others. Ruth Heflin and Calvary Campground, Steve Hill and the Brownsville Revival and others, like Joan Giesen, sowed into my life. As you walk together and work together with men and women of God, they leave a deposit on your life that is eternal.

Paul talked of this in his writings. He had a proper relationship with those who had poured into his life, but he was also careful to maintain a good relationship with those who would carry on after he was gone. For instance, Paul walked with peers like Silas and Barnabas, and he was also careful to maintain his relationship with the apostolic council in Jerusalem, where James was in charge. That was the older generation. At the same time, however, he was pouring into younger men like Titus and Timothy, his spiritual sons. Having the several generations working together in unity and harmony is the ideal.

The great shaking that has been taking place over the last few years all over the world has a divine purpose. Everything God does is with purpose and order. He is shaking us now and everything that can be shaken will be shaken. The goal is that what is pure Kingdom will remain. God is bringing forth a great Kingdom alignment, a generational alignment, a spiritual authority alignment, so that we can properly relate to the other parts of His Body.

This was the picture the psalmist was trying to portray in Psalm 133, when he spoke of the precious anointing oil running down the priest's body and onto his garments:

Behold, how good and how pleasant it is
For brethren to dwell together in unity!

It is like the precious oil upon the head,
Running down on the beard,
The beard of Aaron,
Running down on the edge of his garments.
It is like the dew of Hermon,
Descending upon the mountains of Zion;
For there the LORD commanded the blessing—
Life forevermore.   Psalm 133:1-3, NKJV

In just this way, there is a spiritual alignment taking place today, putting men and women into right relationship and giving them the ability to walk with, work with and receive from many who are destined to pour into their lives.

Again, Paul wrote to the Corinthian believers:

> *For though ye have ten thousand instructers in Christ, yet have ye not many fathers: for in Christ Jesus I have begotten you through the gospel.* 1 Corinthians 4:15

We need a fresh revelation of spiritual paternity and maternity because this is an hour in which the hearts of the fathers are being turned again to the children and the children back to their parents. These things are coming into play as we move from generation to generation, and a new breed of end-time warriors and handmaidens come on the scene.

It is so important that we get the prophetic view and vision of the heart of God, so that we can make the transitions He requires in a way that is pleasing to Him and that brings Him glory. To me, this is one of the major things we have not done well in the Body of

Christ—raising up the next generation, preparing them, equipping them and then launching them into their destiny. This requires releasing them and then working with them, reaping the harvest together.

This race we are in is not a sprint. It is not a marathon. It is actually a relay race, and it includes participants from several generations. Oh, how important it is that we get this revelation of how the Christian ministry is to operate.

Personally, I have never felt comfortable working alone. I have always wanted a team to work with me, and I have been blessed from the beginning to have just such a wonderful team. However, as I have traveled and visited hundreds of churches through the years, I have found that far too many pastors struggle with this concept and have no workable plan in effect for transitioning their ministry to the next generation. It has been my privilege to work on both sides of this issue, ministering to those who are now being released into their destiny and also to those who are now passing on their blessing. This is a critical moment, one in which we desperately need to be ready to pass the baton to a new generation.

In a sprint, like the hundred-yard dash, there is no baton. A solo runner wins or loses on his or her own merit. There is no passing of the baton. The Christian life and ministry, however, are more like the relay race. No one runs alone. No one wins alone, and no one loses alone. We're all in this together.

For those who have never run a relay race, it involves a baton that is passed from one runner to the next. Each team has several runners. No one person runs the entire race. Each one takes his or her turn doing a certain portion of the race. Running fast and well is important, but just as important is how the baton is passed from one runner to the next. If this is not done well, the whole team is slowed down or eliminated altogether.

In a relay race, the fastest runner doesn't always win. Each team is credited with the combined speeds of its runners (minus the time it takes them to hand off the baton from runner to runner). So a slow runner or one who does the pass-off of the baton poorly can cause his or her team to lose.

In many relay races, there are four runners per team, and each of these team members must be carefully chosen. Since one can drag down the whole team, each of them is equally important.

One of the fastest runners is often placed to go first. That way, the team can get a head start on the other competing teams. This decision is made by a coach who has been working with the runners and knows them well. He has a strategy for winning, and everyone on the team must trust him and follow his strategy.

The second runner may be what is called a "pace runner," one who holds the line. He or she is very diligent and will not allow another runner to overtake and pass them. Therefore, the lead gained by the first runner is maintained.

The final runner, of course, is also extremely important. Here you want someone who will pull out all the stops and make a heroic effort to reach the finish line first. This final runner, very often, determines the difference between winning and losing, but, in truth, it takes all four runners working together, cooperating with each other, doing their individual best, but also contributing to the whole, to take home the prize.

There are many dynamics at play here, and I want to elaborate on a few of them and compare them with the race you and I are running today for the Lord. Paul spoke of this race when he wrote:

> *I have fought a good fight, I have finished my course, I have kept the faith: henceforth there is laid up for me a crown of righteousness, which the Lord, the righteous judge, shall give me at that day: and not to me only, but unto all them also that love his appearing.* 2 Timothy 6:7-8

Paul ran the race assigned to him, finishing his course, and I'm sure that you also want to finish well in this Christian life and ministry. I do too.

Part of finishing well is developing and passing on a proper legacy. That is the only way we can live on after we are gone. What does this involve? It involves birthing sons and daughters into the faith, equipping and empowering them and then launching them forth. If the baton is never placed in their hands, what contribution can they make to the race? If our spiritual sons and daughters are not raised up and then put into the race and supported, whose fault is it? They can only run their leg of the race as you enable them to do so.

There are several crucial elements to the relay race, and none of them can be ignored. Speed, clearly, is one of them. Each runner must run well. If not, they will surely be replaced by another.

Endurance is a second crucial element of winning. If a runner is fast but tires easily, other competing runners may well overtake them, and the whole team will suffer. Practice endurance and teach endurance to others.

But speed and endurance are not enough. A third critical element is timing, specifically the timing of passing the baton. It sounds easy, but it is one of the most difficult parts of the race.

To perform this part of the race successfully requires relationship. You must know your partner and know how they think and how they react. The two of you must be in sync. Can you trust him? Can he trust you? There must be a mutual trust for this part of the race to be successful.

The two runners are not looking at each other. Each is concentrated on his or her particular responsibility, but they now begin moving together in unison. The race is often won or lost in fractions of a second or, at best, a few seconds, so the least little thing that goes wrong at this point can cause a serious problem. Passing or receiving the baton well or not can easily win or lose the race for your team.

When a runner is approaching the area of passing the baton, the next runner cannot just stand there looking on. They must begin moving too. You can never wait for the other person to get there. It's too late then. For the pass to take place successfully, both runners must be moving at a similar speed.

Now (and this is important) the active runner must slow down a little. The pass does not take place at breakneck speed. If the first runner has to come to a standstill, then the momentum is lost, and another team will pass you by. So the second runner must be in position, must be concentrating on the right timing and must start moving, in order to get up his momentum and meet the first runner in the allocated space. The first runner must slow down a little and must coordinate a smooth handoff to his partner or all is lost.

I mentioned the allocated space, and that is so important. The runners cannot just hookup wherever they want. There is a marked box with beginning and ending boundaries. They cannot hand off the baton before they get to the first line of that box, and they cannot wait to pass off the baton until they have passed the second line.

This box is known as the "transfer zone," and it is critical to the race strategy. Merely passing the baton is not enough. It must be passed in the proper timing. There is a time and place for everything.

In the relay race, there are certain things that can disqualify you. If you drop the baton anywhere along the way, there is a very good chance that you will be disqualified. If you fail to pass the baton to the next runner, you will most certainly be disqualified. If you pass the baton but not within the clearly marked area, you will be disqualified and/or penalized. Coordination, cooperation and teamwork is everything in this race.

When the second runner begins to run, he is looking forward, but his hand is extended backward, toward his partner, ready and able to receive the baton. Otherwise, how can the first runner pass it off?

The second runner begins to run, then picks up speed. It is then that the first runner slows a little … until both runners are running at the same speed, and the handoff can take place. When they have reached the transfer box, that's the moment of truth. Can the first runner hand off the baton without dropping it or stumbling? Can the second runner receive the baton and then move quickly to full speed without dropping it? The moment the second runner feels that baton in his hand, he can then quickly turn on the burners and push himself to top speed, but not a moment before.

Now, even as the second runner accelerates, the first runner is slowing down further, cooling off and eventually coming to a full stop. Which of these runners is the most important? Neither is more important than the other. They are of equal importance. They are members of a team, and it is the team that either wins or loses. If that bothers a runner, then he or she cannot participate in this type of race.

For a few moments, the two runners were running together, at the same speed, but just until the baton is passed in the transfer box. Then, BOOM!, the transfer of authority and power has suddenly taken place, and the race has changed. It can all take place in a moment of time, when everything comes together as it should.

If I have the baton in my hand, I can then say to myself, "It's mine," and I can take it and run with it, accelerating my speed and beginning my successful leg of the race. I now have to concentrate on not dropping the baton, on maintaining my speed and my endurance and staying in my own lane.

During most races, staying in your own lane is very important. Personally, I have seen many Christians fail because of getting out of their lane, out of their gifting, calling and area of ministry. It happens because people want what others have or begin comparing themselves to others and not being satisfied with what God has given them. Stay in your lane. Stay in your stream and know who you are running with. Understand those who run before you and get in sync with them, not through blind faith, but through a healthy relationship.

My spiritual sons and daughters and I have developed a rock-solid trust. If I tell one of them to meet me at a certain address at a certain time in a particular city, I can trust them to be there (and on time). We must become people of trust, and we must become totally trustworthy, men and women of our word. Love one another, and trust one another.

For many years now, I have run this race to the fullest of my ability, but I sense that I am coming around a turn in life, and I am getting ready to pass the baton to the next runner. I can see them now afar off and when I get nearer, I will slow a little, to allow them to move into position to receive my pass.

That teammate will run the next leg, so as they see me coming, they will begin to move into place and pick up speed. Now we must both pace ourselves, running stride for stride, so as to achieve the pass-off in the right timing and location.

I could spoil the race by deciding that I no longer wish to hand off the baton. I'm having too much fun in the race. But that's not how it works. I am part of a team and my Coach (Jesus) decides who runs the next leg. I have had my chance. Hopefully I have done my best, and now I will trust my teammate to do their best too.

As the person responsible for handing off the baton, I don't expect my running mate to be looking back. I am looking ahead, watching their hand, timing myself to place the baton in that hand at the proper time. When I deem it to be the right time, BOOM! the transfer takes place. No time has been lost, the baton was not dropped, and the transfer took place before we left the box. The next runner can now spring forward and race to the finish line.

At first, I was running. Then we were both running together. Then, out of courtesy for my partner, I slowed down a little so that the transfer could take place. Now the baton is safely in the hands of another, and I can cool down and then rest.

The Christian race is all about family. You want to be treated with respect, so you must treat the other members of the family with respect. You want others to recognize your importance in the race, so you must recognize their importance in the race. You want others to walk with you and work with you, so you must walk with them and work with them.

The whole team waits until the last leg of the race has been finished, and then you all celebrate that great moment together. You have respected each other. You have paced yourselves. Each one has done his best and then successfully passed the baton to the next generation. You have trusted each other. You have stayed strong in the good times and bad, working together in unity and harmony. Now it's time to rejoice.

The baton has been passed to a new generation. It must not be dropped. These new runners must be there for one another, cheering each other on and awaiting their team's victory and their team's celebration.

Everything Jesus did during His time on the Earth was about preparing and launching a new generation. Now it's our turn. Let us *"press toward the mark for the prize of the high calling of God in Christ Jesus"* (Philippians 3:14). The prize we strive for is not carnal. It *"fadeth not away"* (1 Peter 1:4).

Oh how I appreciate the wonderful men and women God has sent into my life over the years. I hope they learned a few things from me. I have learned a lot from them. This is *The Art of Legacy*.

NOW IT'S OUR TURN TO RUN THE RACE. LET US PRESS TOWARD THE MARK FOR THE HIGH CALLING OF GOD IN CHRIST JESUS!

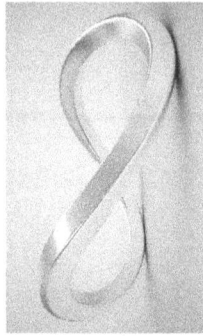

Chapter 13

What Now? What's Next?

I believe that we have entered into the greatest season in the history of the Church, the season that every prophet prophesied about, the season of the greatest battle ever known to man and also the greatest harvest ever known to man. In the year 2020, we took a giant step into end-time prophecy being fulfilled—days of war and roses.

In the natural, we experienced a pandemic that has presented us with the greatest crisis of our generation. Yet this moment in time is pregnant with opportunity. It seemed that in a moment's time life as we know it came to a standstill. I believe that the enemy orchestrated and brought this upon mankind. But those of us who understand the goodness and mercy and grace of God know *"that all things work together for good to those who love God, to those who are the called according to His purpose."* (Romans 8:28, NKJV). The Lord will use this moment for our good and for His glory.

This is a moment in time that the Spirit of the Lord will use for a giant reset. His love for us is beyond description, without limit or bounds, and not based on our performance, but on His goodness. He could not be happy with the present condition of His Church, His Bride. When He brings us correction, it is to verify our legitimacy as sons and daughters and confirm His love for us. We are in that moment of the restoration of all things, and He is bringing forth perfect spiritual alignment.

In coming out of this season, the worst thing that can happen to us, individually and collectively, is that we come out in the same condition we were in when we entered it. God is looking for His Kingdom leaders, spiritual mentors, to re-establish Kingdom culture. He wants us to demonstrate both a family and a Kingdom model, revealing and dealing with problem issues of the past as well as unveiling the new. He is calling us to a deep season of intimacy and relationship because those who know their God will do mighty exploits (see Daniel 11:32).

The season that now lies ahead of us is a season of signs, wonders and miracles and the gifts of the Spirit, a season of entering a deeper place of the supernatural realm, the Glory realm of God. Therefore, He is bringing forth a deep awareness of our true identity as sons and daughters, so that we can restore identity to our society in the midst of transformation. He is training and preparing the army of God, as well as demonstrating that true family model of the local church with a Kingdom purpose. He is restoring the tabernacle of David in His quest for us to worship Him in Spirit and in truth. He is purging us and cleansing us with His fire, to bring forth the gold and the silver, a pure Bride, without spot or wrinkle, demonstrating character and integrity and worshiping Him in the beauty of holiness.

This is a season that we must yield to the Spirit of God and experience a true Kingdom reset, changing us from a Church mindset to a Kingdom mindset that begins at the very foundation of Kingdom alignment in Matthew 6:33:

What Now? What's Next?

But seek ye first the kingdom of God, and his righteousness; and all these things shall be added unto you.

Change can only occur as we allow the Spirit of God to challenge and confront our present condition. We must personally and corporately enter into a season of heartfelt repentance, bathed in tears, bringing forth with joy in the morning and bearing fruit of legitimate change. We must embrace our true calling, emulating the ministry of Christ, the ministry of reconciliation and restoration, demonstrating true spiritual family values of fatherhood and sonship, discipling and mentoring the next generation and launching them into their destiny, thus leaving a spiritual legacy.

We must be ready to confront evil, bring forth justice and deal with the issues we are faced with in a bold, honest and forthright manner, walking and working together in unity and harmony, generation to generation. This is *The Art of Legacy*.

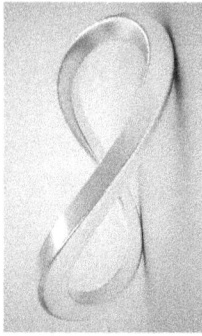

Legacy

In the Kingdom we walk forward
With love for one another,
Being willing to live and die
For our sisters and our brothers.

Time goes quickly by,
And our children sing legacy's song.
And before we know it
They carry us along.

We look ahead in love,
Remembering generations gone by,
And reflect on all the godly things
That serve as an eternal tie.

They bind us together
With our future and the past,
And they tell a beautiful story
That will endure and last.

Legacy

We are all God's children,
A "chosen generation,"
A "royal priesthood" unto Jesus,
A pure and "holy nation."

We remember and treasure the memories
Of lives we've lived and shared,
The way we walked together,
The way we loved and cared.

We remember tears and laughter,
Our mutual joys and sorrows.
We embrace all our yesterdays
And look forward to tomorrows.

We retrace our footsteps
And all our hopes and aspirations.
We remember all that's come and gone
Throughout the generations.

Every year has been a gift
God has given us to use.
Hours and days waiting to be filled
In any way we choose.

The Art of Legacy

Lord, every new season
Brings faith restored, renewed,
Wrapped in expectant hope,
Fulfilled in trusting You.

Every new tomorrow
Brings abundant life and grace
And opportunities to truly rise
And run and win our race.

As we turn our hearts to the children,
And their hearts are turned as well,
We will walk in the fulness of Your promise.
And Your purpose our lives will tell.

And, as the seasons come and go
With lightning acceleration,
We'll thank God we've worked to pass the baton
From generation to generation. ♥

Mave Moyer

Author Contact Page

You may contact the author in the following ways:

By Email
bro.russ@eagleworldwide.com

By Phone:
+1 905 308 9991

By Mail:
PO Box 39
Copetown ON L0R1J0
Canada

On Facebook:

facebook.com/eagleworldwide

facebook.com/russ.moyer.52

By visiting his website:
www.EagleWorldwide.com

EAGLE WORLDWIDE
RETREAT & REVIVAL CENTRE

SUMMER CAMP TENT REVIVAL

July through August
8 Powerful Weeks of Revival
Every Night @ 7:00 pm

Specialty Schools
School of the Prophets
School of Freedom and Healing
School of the Supernatural

Location: 976 Hwy 52 Copetown ON L0R 1J0
Call for more details 905 308 9991
www.EagleWorldwide.com

WINTER CAMP REVIVAL GLORY

February/March
10 Powerful Days of Revival Glory
Every Night @ 7:00 pm

Specialty Schools
School of the Prophets

The Dwelling Place
7895 Pensacola Blvd Pensacola FL 32534
Call for more details 850 473 8255
www.TheDwellingPlaceChurch.org